The Fearless Classroom

Students learn better when they aren't afraid to take risks and make mistakes. In this book, teacher and popular blogger Joli Barker shows you how to make K-8 students fearless in the classroom so they can engage in deeper learning. You'll discover how to abandon the notion of the teacher as the primary source of information, and instead create a classroom environment in which students can explore problems, test theories, and play games through curiosity, imagination, adaptability, and a passion for learning.

Find out how to…

- Create fearless learning environments;
- Engage in fearless planning and lesson design;
- Use fearless grading and assessments;
- Teach fearless gamification;
- Develop fearless parent relations; and
- Get students to ask fearless questions.

Throughout the book, you'll find suggested activities for science, social studies, language arts, and math, as well as tools such as rubrics to assist you on your journey.

Joli Barker is an elementary teacher in Texas. She is Microsoft in Education Master Educator and Global Forum winner. She was the 2013 Texas Computer Education Association's Classroom Teacher of the Year. She is also one of The National School Board Association's 2014 "20 to Watch" in education. She has a popular blog, The Fearless Classroom, and also does consulting work in schools.

The Fearless Classroom

A Practical Guide to Experiential Learning Environments

Joli Barker

Routledge
Taylor & Francis Group

NEW YORK AND LONDON

First published 2015
by Routledge
711 Third Avenue, New York, NY 10017

and by Routledge
2 Park Square, Milton Park, Abingdon, Oxon, OX14 4RN

Routledge is an imprint of the Taylor & Francis Group, an informa business

© 2015 Taylor & Francis

Library of Congress Cataloging in Publication Data
    Barker, Joli.
The fearless classroom : a practical guide to experiential learning environments /
Joli Barker.
        pages cm
    1. Teaching.   2. Learning, Psychology of.   3. Classroom environment.   I. Title.
    LC1025.B37 2014
    371.102—dc23
    2014013324

ISBN: 978-1-138-80285-8 (hbk)
ISBN: 978-1-138-80286-5 (pbk)
ISBN: 978-1-315-75400-0 (ebk)

Typeset in Minion Pro
by Apex CoVantage, LLC

Printed and bound in the United States of America by Publishers Graphics, LLC on sustainably sourced paper.

DEDICATION

This book is dedicated to all of my teachers, both young and old, who continue to influence me to fearlessly live my passions and dream ever bigger.

To Anthony, thank you for your unfailing faith in me.

To Mom and Dad, thank you for teaching me to always believe in the power of love and determination.

. . . and most of all . . .

To Nick and Jaden, my genius sons, you are my greatest teachers of all. I love you with all that I am.

MEET THE AUTHOR

Joli Barker has been teaching for almost twenty years in both secondary and elementary classrooms. She has been recognized as a leader in education by the National School Board Association's 20 to Watch Program, Microsoft Expert Educator Program, and Discovery Education Network. She is a member of ISTE and was named the Texas Computer Education Association's Teacher of the Year in 2013. Her passion for innovation in the 21st-century classroom has propelled her to the top of her field and has earned her the respect of her colleagues on a global platform.

CONTENTS

NOTE FROM THE AUTHOR

The best teacher is the one who suggests rather than dogmatizes,
and inspires his listener with the wish to teach himself.
—EDWARD BULWER-LYTTON

When I was an elementary student, my curiosity about my world and what I was learning was always left unsatisfied. I wondered, as I completed the math drills and diagramming of sentences, "Why do I need to know this? When will I ever need to use this?" When I learned about geography, the places about which I was learning were nothing more than fantastic wisps of information. I had no connections to the curriculum and my own life experiences. I believed that school was only a necessary obstacle to adulthood.

Though I struggled as a reader, I was clever enough to make strong grades and to graduate in the top 10 percent of my class. Still, I never saw a connection to the real world and what I was learning. My education was nothing more than a contrived effort to please a teacher and was significantly short of authentic learning.

In fourth grade I met the teacher who would be the first to change my life. Mr Joshua believed in me though my shyness and insecurity was almost debilitating. He encouraged me, celebrated me, highlighted my abilities, and lit the spark in me to believing in myself. It was the first time I saw learning and school as something to enjoy and something I could do for myself.

In seventh grade I met the second teacher who would show me that teachers cared about us as people. Coach Murff created a science class filled with laughter, experiential learning, and commitment to making sure that we all understood the concepts he was teaching.

Even back in 1987, he was a teacher who believed in allowing students to collaborate and experience learning.

In tenth grade I met my last of my K-12 teachers who would influence me to teach. Mr Christian, my calculus teacher, taught me that games could be powerful learning tools. He made learning fun and effortless.

And because of these extraordinary educators, I applied to college to become a teacher. It wasn't until my sophomore year, however, that I discovered the power of innovative teaching. It wasn't until I attended my American Literature course in college that I was finally introduced to 100 percent authentic learning. The historical significance of and influences behind the fictional storylines and characters of which we were studying illuminated the darkened and neglected part of my belief system about education. What I had always thought was shattered. A new life was breathed into my desire to learn and, at nineteen years old, I became, for the first time in my life, a student.

When I decided to become an educator, I wanted not only to make a difference in the lives of children, but in my community also. I wanted to ensure that every child that graced my classroom doorway would leave with a firm understanding of why and how the curriculum could be used in his or her life. I wanted to tear down the walls and expose my students to the world—*their* world—and the world of endless opportunities. I wanted to teach them that regardless of their age, economic situation, or ability level, they could succeed in making a difference in their own lives and their community.

I believe that the two most important jobs on earth are being a parent and teacher. I take my role as both extremely seriously and approach my classroom as a way to extend the "family" for my students. I encourage parent participation through technology and visits to the classroom, utilize their "expertise" in virtual and on-site field trips, and teach as I would want my own children taught: with respect, encouragement, and the conviction to continuously motivate students to raise their own bars and fan the flame of intrinsic learning within themselves. I often quote arguably one of the most influential and inspirational educators in history, Anne Sullivan, who said, "My heart is singing for joy this morning! A miracle has happened! The light of understanding has shone upon my little pupil's mind, and behold, all things are changed!" This perfectly expresses the mood and focus of my classroom daily. This is truly what my work is all about.

Joli Barker

PREFACE

Defining Fearlessness

Traditional teaching methods might appear to have become transformed into new pedagogy and techniques, but are we really just repackaging the same ineffective ideas in new, more expensive digital wrapping? Arguably we are. What is preventing us from becoming an educational juggernaut that sets the global standard in education? Why are we more focused on data and standards than the pathway to knowledge acquisition? How can we relinquish our fears and embrace this new way of thinking and teaching? We must first define what it means to be fearless.

What It Means to be Fearless

The key to change . . . is to let go of fear.
—Rosanne Cash

As educators, we are torn between wanting to educate children to be thinkers, explorers, and curious souls, and covering the curriculum to the expectation levels set by our campus, district, or state. Being fearless means taking a leap of faith, a well-calculated risk, that the curriculum is secondary to the education you will be providing. It is believing that you, the teacher, are actually the weakest source of information you could give to your student, but the most powerful of idea-generators, question-posers, genius-cultivators, and that, in fact, the students are capable of learning without you. We must allow failure to always be an option in our classrooms. By embracing the mindset that fearlessness is not just another approach but rather a new pedagogical perspective, we can commit to fail, disappoint, and make mistakes eagerly.

We must fail to stop learning, fail to become complacent, fail to be satisfied with our work. Our world changes at a rate faster than technology ever thought about, yet so many teachers continue to "do what worked last year" simply because it worked last year. We should always think, "New moment, new student, new opportunity to grow." We are not teaching today's students to function in today's career fields, because today's careers will be obsolete tomorrow. Rather we must educate our students to be prepared to adapt and change for future careers that have yet to be created.

We must disappoint those who truly believe that "Those who can do, and those who can't teach." We must rise above the naysayers and those who would have us be less than we are and can be. Disappoint anyone who argues that there isn't an art to extraordinary teaching and that our educational system is being left behind by the rest of the world.

Finally, we *must* make mistakes. Make them daily . . . in front of our students . . . and let them engage in solutions *with* us. It is a necessary tool in learning to struggle through a challenge in order to find authentic learning. Model that it is okay to make mistakes, to get do-overs, to keep trying and failing and trying again. In this world of instant gratification *this* alone is one of the greatest gifts we can give our students.

We are held to expectations that can, at times, seem overwhelming and unfair. But if we set expectations for ourselves that surpass those which our state and district set for us . . . if we hold ourselves accountable to the much higher standards our students deserve . . . then there really is nothing to prevent us from inspiring greatness and recognizing that moment to fan the flame of learning.

How to Prepare for the Fearless Revolution

In order to truly transform the educational environment in our classrooms, we must abandon what we feel is comfortable and safe, and consider the end goal in a new light. We should be open-minded and open-hearted, and willing to make teaching a way of life. Truly we must hold fast to the belief that *all* children deserve extraordinary educational opportunities that are readily available if we just provide the environment in which students can explore, be curious and imaginative, and thrive. Cape yourself with the superpower gifts all good educators are blessed to have: a steadfast desire to improve the lives of children and their future, and a passion to see them succeed that trumps all criticism, frustration, and doubt.

To be the educator in a fearless classroom one must insist upon constant, perpetual, and unwavering curiosity from oneself and one's students. If they aren't curious about the content in your class . . . be afraid . . . be very afraid.

Are *you* ready? They are.

FOREWORD

A Beacon of Hope and Bravery

For the past several years, I have had the privilege nearly every day to look through a virtual window into the wondrous world of the fearless classroom.

I've never actually visited McKinney, Texas, but anyone can experience the fearless classroom, from anywhere. This is because no educator gives more of herself, and shares more liberally and insightfully, than Joli Barker.

The book you're holding in your hand (or reading on a screen) will change your life, leaving you braver and more hopeful than you've ever been. You'll never "finish" it—you, too, will want to continue to drink in the fearless classroom each and every day.

I often post provocative tweets on Twitter, or the "Genius Question of the Day" on Facebook. These were originally intended to foment an enriching virtual discussion amongst the thousands of passionate educators that I'm blessed to collaborate with online. Some posts work better than others, and rarely does the discussion rise to the level of being unforgettable.

At least, that was the case before the fearless classroom began to participate.

While they have indeed provoked scores of memorable and enriching discussions, the most breathtaking comments have come from one third-grade classroom in McKinney, Texas. With Joli's leadership, these students are intrepid, determined, and fully living up and into their genius.

Wherever I go, I describe a typical 5-year-old: audacious, passionate, energetic, and 100 percent confident that he or she can change the world. By second grade, only about 90 percent of students still feel this way. By the end of fourth grade, it plunges to about 60 percent.

But I am highly confident that nearly all students fortunate enough to experience the fearless classroom in third grade carry with them the audacity of a 5-year-old for many years hence.

The brilliant thoughts that emanate from her classroom lay down roots in my mind. When talking with people who I know have read them and understood their power, they have become legendary quotes that we refer to again and again.

"We are Gen—I—US."

"My brave is my song."

"I never knew I could be someone's hope."

When I asked the world "How Big is Your Brave," Joli responded, "My BRAVE is LARGE and abundant because being fearless has led me to some extraordinary experiences so far!"

Her geniuses pitched in:

"Being fearless is tough sometimes. I still get scared, but when I decide to push through it I always end up feeling a little braver than before."

"My bravery is really big because I am fearless. Not fearless as in having no fears, just fearless in that I don't let fears stop me."

"I am brave when I go on stage to sing in front of a lot of people. I am strong and courageous. My brave is my song."

Each morning, I ask my "Genius Question of the Day" on Facebook. I usually get a few answers, but not as many as you'd expect to a simple question asked of 4,600 adults. This is because most adults struggle with recognizing, accepting, and living up and into their genius.

One day I asked, "Am I Serving as Only I Can Serve?"

This received more answers than usual, because the fearless classroom weighed in. Here is how they responded:

"Yes because I prayed with my mom this morning because she was having a really bad morning."

"Yes, because I am a really good reader and I helped a friend learn a new way to remember the important stuff."

"No, but I will be now. I sometimes forget that I have something special to give to people. But I remember now. I can be a really good friend."

"Yes, because I walked with a friend to school in the rain and held his umbrella for him so he wouldn't drop his stuff."

"Yes because I try to smile at other kids in our school when we are in the hallway. Smiles always make me feel better so I figure if I smile then they will feel happy too."

"Yes because I am a genius and you are helping us use what we are learning in class to help others. I feel really good about helping people. Before this year, I didn't think I could actually be someone's hope."

Joli is not only the hope for her students in the fearless classroom. She is also hope for many. For teachers, who become brave because of her model. For parents, Joli is a reminder of what to look for in their own child's teacher and school. For administrators, who see passion like this in action in their own buildings. For the world, who on the worst of days can go to her blog, Facebook postings, and Twitter stream to remind themselves of what really matters.

For me, I am braver and wiser because of Joli and her genius learners.

And for you dear reader, let this book be your beacon of hope and bravery. Let it be a reminder of who *you* are and how much your genius is needed by your students and the world.

You matter!

Angela Maiers
Nationally recognized speaker and consultant on
21st-century teaching, and co-author of
The Passion-Driven Classroom

Defining Fearlessness

You can catch more flies with honey than vinegar.
—AMERICAN PROVERB

The Fearless Educator

As educators, we want what is best for our students. We also tend to teach how we have learned, through traditional teaching. Sure, we have come a long way from the old "lecture only, students in rows" kind of pedagogy, but consumptive learning is still the preferred method of most teachers. But as life has a special way of teaching us, our greatest lessons are often learned through adversity. So why, then, are we afraid to allow students to struggle and fail? We love them, that's why! We want so much for understanding to happen for our students that we sometimes inadvertently can be the obstacles that prevent students from experiencing true learning. Our good intentions block the authentic learning from happening. I often tell my students that if they knew everything I had planned for them to learn then they would not be in my class. I want them to know that it is okay to say, "I don't know," as long as it is followed with, "but I can certainly learn it!" I want them to feel comfortable with struggle and failure, knowing that these are necessary steps to a deeper understanding and most certainly to a moment of self-confidence in achievement. I am their advocate, their facilitator, and their safety net. I am there to offer guidance but not answers, encouragement but not coddling.

Educators today must let go of the idea that they must be the sole provider of information and that all activities to reinforce that information need to be practice and consumptive. There is much research to show that discovery activities and challenging problem-solving activities that require collaboration and communication between students are more powerful in creating deeper learning than passive, consumptive activities. It is a beautiful thing to have a busy, engaged, lively classroom versus a quiet classroom. Students need to learn to communicate their thinking, negotiate learning from each other, and collaboratively engage in learning with other students. Fearless educators understand that functioning as more of a safety net and clarifier for students offers more opportunities for authentic intervention within the context of the learning activity rather than pulling students into isolated and more contrived small-group learning activities.

The Fearless Student

It is true that we educators should approach our responsibilities to our students fearlessly and that they, as students of the world, should approach their learning fearlessly. But there is another layer to the idea of a fearless classroom. As I walk the hallways of elementary schools around our collective communities, I often hear the following statements echoing within the walls of the schools, which are even more concerning in the hearts of the kids who learn there.

"You need to do your best on this test or you may have to repeat this grade."

"If you don't start working harder the next grade level is going to be even more difficult!"

"You need to sit down and be quiet! There is *no talking* in this classroom."

"If you don't get to work you will not have recess!"

I cringe when I hear those comments. Why do we feel that it is more effective to scare students into submission or conformity than to encourage them to do the right thing and have integrity in their work?

What if our principal were to conduct an observation of one of our lessons? And what if he or she came up to us after the lesson and said, "You're not getting a contract next year because you didn't try on that lesson"?

I know how I would feel. I'd feel defeated, then I'd get mad, then I would lose faith in him or her as a leader, and I would stop caring about what he or she had to say. I might decide to leave and go to another school, but, if I was cut from a different cloth, I might decide that I was not a good teacher and I would quit. I believe that I am no different than any other human. We all like to have praise for our efforts; recognition for the hard work we put in. Some of us need it more than others, but we all like it. So, perhaps a more accurate question would be, "How could we encourage students to do the right thing and to have integrity in their work?" How can we foster a classroom culture where students put their names on their work not because it is simply a means of identifying one's work, or because it is an expectation of the teacher, but because they *want* to stake claim to the incredible effort that the work represents?

So how do we create a fearless classroom in these terms? How do we create a culture of supportive encouragement, praise, and validation?

The greatest barrier to success is the fear of failure.
—SVEN-GÖRAN ERIKSSON

Students respond to success much more readily than they do to failure. Behaviorally, the same sentiment rings true. We want children to find a competitive spark within themselves to set their own expectations and goals, and to work feverishly to achieve those goals. One of the ways I have successfully evoked this kind of climate in my classroom is to spend a few moments at the beginning of each day having students set their own academic goals. I keep them constantly informed of their academic achievements and areas of opportunity so that they can assess and evaluate for themselves what they need to do to reach their goals. At the beginning of the year, this is quite a teach piece, but by midyear they are exceptional at assessing their needs and writing reasonable and attainable goals for themselves. Additionally, through gamification, students are immersed in high scores, "unlock-able" achievements, and level-ups, which add an engaging layer of commitment to producing their highest-quality work.

Another way I cultivate a fearless classroom is to always praise, even when disciplining or offering critical feedback. I praise effort and encourage brainstorming and risk-taking. When a student volunteers an inaccurate answer, I praise the contribution because it facilitates a discussion that leads to deeper learning. Without that student taking the risk and offering that inaccurate answer, the learning that takes place as a result might never have happened. So we celebrate it. This also provides that risk-taker with a pat on the back for trying, thus increasing the likelihood that he or she will try again. It instills a sense of fearless tenacity and determination to persevere.

If you were to visit my classroom and ask my students if they were scared or worried about the next grade, the state test, or their future, they would emphatically let you know that not only are they prepared, but also that they are excited about what the future holds for them. I want to make sure that this point is clearly stated: I do not fill them with ego-boosting coddling of empty compliments that have no valid-ity to them. This isn't about filling students with so much praise that they have a false sense of grandeur or arrogance. This is about helping students discover the genius within each of them and helping them realize that each of them has a gift that the world simply *must* experience.

Together, my students have developed the use of the cultural ver-nacular of OMG and LOL and BRB, which they coined to mean "Observing Major Genius," "Love Our Learning," and "Be Right-Brained," respectively. The kids believe in themselves and compete only with their own accomplishments. We are a family that supports each other and will work together to make sure that truly no child is left behind.

Preparing students for school is far less important than preparing them for life. They need to feel that they can accomplish anything but that sometimes that means a lot of hard work and it may take years before they realize their success. They need to believe in their abilities and potential, and to have frequent and consistent experiences with struggle, failure, and improving reattempts. They need to know that every moment, every experience, is an opportunity to learn and that they should embrace it with wonder and eagerness.

Scaring kids into performing on a test, or working independently, or being quiet or anything else is not only counter-productive, but also can actually set them up for failure that they are not going to be able to handle effectively and which could potentially destroy their ambitions to succeed.

The impossible often has a kind of integrity which the merely improbable lacks.

—Douglas Adams

Students of all ages need to believe that what they are doing matters. In every context, throughout every content and activity, what they are doing must matter to them, or they will never understand that integrity falls squarely on their shoulders. And that their work, no matter how minute or mundane it may seem, is crucial to their development as a significant person in this world. It is our job to help form those connections from one concept to another. We must help them discover how what they have done in previous grades or lessons were all precursors to what they are doing now, and how what they are doing now will ultimately help them find success down the line. But more important than any of that is this: We as educators must foster the idea that nothing is impossible when great minds believe in possibilities. Failure must become a welcome stepping-stone to success rather than a barrier. Many educators believe that failure can destroy self-esteem and the willingness to take future risks. So how do we do this? How do we help our students discover the "I'm Possible" within themselves?

First of all, just telling kids that they are incredible and that you believe in them is no longer enough. Kids are smart enough to pick up on lip service. We can be the kindest, most supportive teachers in the game and still have kids feeling unworthy of praise, incapable of success, and unwilling to try. Why is this? It is because we are the teachers and we present ourselves as the primary source of information and therefore know just about everything there is to know about everything. "Because I said so" can be readily used when we really don't know, but what does that say to the kids? I try to interject something new into every class period—something new that I have never done before either. I call it my Genius Table and we work through the activities together. They see me struggle, adapt, adjust my strategies and thinking, fail, fail, fail, fail, fail, fail . . . fail, try again and again . . . and sometimes still end up unsuccessful. That is until I *am* successful. Maybe it is a Sudoku problem, or a Mensa question, or a new task like needlepoint or even a tough jigsaw puzzle. Anything will do as long as none of us has a clue as to how to accomplish the task.

Their faces light up when they get farther in the task than I do. But even more impressive is the look on their faces when their "genius, award-winning teacher" struggles and fails right along with them. She doesn't get upset, she doesn't quit, and she doesn't feel sorry for herself. She laughs, thinks, talks to them, and asks them for advice and help. *This* is where true learning happens. *This* is when the impossible becomes "I'm Possible."

> *Believe and act as if it were impossible to fail.*
> —Charles F. Kettering

When a child believes that there is no such thing as failure, that every unsuccessful trial is simply data for how to succeed, then failure truly loses its power over them. They embrace it. They long for it. They know that if they are failing now it only means that they are getting closer to the solution. Students need to experience this feeling and feel it fully every single day. It starts, though, with you. You have to let go of the fear that a less than stellar grade somehow reflects poorly on you as the teacher. Take the lackluster academic performances and troubleshoot them with the student. Sit down and discuss item by item what went wrong. Allow them to explain their thinking and how they came to their answer. *Listen.* Take notes. Don't speak other than to smile and say things like, "Ah, yes, I see how you could get that. That's a very interesting and smart thinking process you had!" Say this because indeed it was. Then, in true fearless fashion, send the student back to try again by asking a pointed question like, "What if this question were about (something they are interested in and passionate about like baseball for example)? How might you have answered it then? What if you were to rewrite this question in terms of baseball? How might you answer it then?"

Impossible only means that you haven't found the solution yet.

—MARK TWAIN

Engage students in global conversations. Connect with classrooms within your campus, community, state, country, and internationally. Have these same conversations with other students. Allow your struggling students to discuss and collaborate on solutions to problems with students from other classrooms and schools. We have successfully completed several international projects, which are highlighted later in this book. Students were required to learn from each other, collaborate with other cultures, be patient over time zones, and learn with and from others. What a fantastic way to show new ways of thinking and problem solving with empathy and global mindedness! It truly shows students that anything can be accomplished when we allow ourselves to ask for help and listen respectfully to others.

No one gets very far unless he accomplishes the impossible at least once a day.

—ELBERT HUBBARD

We need to facilitate student perseverance. We must give them frequent and purposeful challenges through which they will struggle, fail, try again, fail, and eventually come to a place where they either successfully find a solution or come close enough to a solution that adequately satisfies their thirst to succeed. We want their passions to be celebrated and taken seriously. We want them approaching their learning with as much determination and vigorous enthusiasm as they do their favorite games or other passions. In the first ten years of my teaching career I heard so frequently the following sentiments echoed in the voices of my students:

"I can't do this."

"I am really bad at math."

"I am not very smart."

"I can't read this."

"Is this right?"

After changing my pedagogy to the fearless classroom approach and making personalized learning activities in my classroom "hard fun," I have since overheard the following comments being made when my students were working on a very rigorous challenge of completing a dot-to-dot based on measurement parameters only:

"This is hard! But I love a challenge!"

"Man! I didn't think I could do this, but look at my picture! I got this!"

"Hey, you're doing great! Measuring is your thing!"

I am convinced that the fearless classroom philosophy is what gives them the confidence to be fearless and enjoy the stepping-stones to success.

The Fearless Approach

There have been extensive scientific studies about how fear and anxiety affect the brain's ability to learn and retain information. In a 2010 study by the National Scientific Council on the Developing Child at Harvard University, *Persistent Fear and Anxiety Can Affect Young Children's Learning and Development*, it was found that if children are exposed to "persistent and chronic anxiety" it can affect the structural makeup of the brain in addition to the developmental processes in the child that deal with learning and memory. However, the anxiety to which the study refers is extreme in nature, such as consistent physical abuse. Obviously, this is far greater an anxiety than children will face in the classroom. We do have to consider the occasional circumstance when this extreme fear and anxiety does occur in our students because they unfortunately may face abuse in their childhoods. But, for the most part, our students are experiencing what most of us might consider typical fear and anxiety about school. After all, we experienced the same fear and anxiety about school ourselves. We worried about tests, getting caught talking or passing notes, getting homework completed, having some infraction documented on our permanent record. We've all been there. What I am suggesting, however, is that even in the brain that faces consistent small doses of the same chemicals released in larger amounts when we are in full frightened state, particularly from the amygdala and the hippocampus, the proportionately similar negative effects on learning and memory take place. Neural pathways become blocked, detoured, or damaged. In other words, a child whose beliefs about his or her learning and classroom environment are anxiety-filled and defeating will experience similar negative effects from the reaction of the brain to that anxiety. For example, long-term memory is affected by the hippocampus. If the hippocampus is under stress by fear and anxiety, how can we expect a student to commit what we are teaching them to long-term memory?

Having said that, some anxiety is a good thing. The anxiety one feels when competing against someone in a race, for example, is a good thing. This kind of anxiety is motivating and propels us forward in our efforts to prevail in the contest. Different chemicals are released and different areas of the brain are activated with this type of anxiety. The brain is a magnificent organ that is still far from understood, but science is making strong progress!

What is even more exciting to think is that our experiences literally create the road map of wiring in our brain. In John Medina's book, *Brain Rules*, he explains that our brains are as unique in structure, storage, and development as our fingerprints. He also describes that emotional stress, especially the stressful feeling of hopelessness or feelings of no control over one's circumstances, is the worst kind of stress on the brain.

The FEAR Factor is recognizing that children who enter our classrooms are Facing Education with Anxiety and Restrictiveness. This is bound to affect their performance in class, especially when faced with taking academic risks or being assessed. As stewards of brain development, teachers must seek to understand how the brain works, how it responds to stimuli with regards to learning and memory, and not just how many facts and procedures the brain can retain and recall at a given moment.

Research by the American Psychological Association shows that fear anxiety adversely affects learning and memory (www.apa.org/education/k12/brain-function.aspx). But it also defines the specific stages of brain development in a child as it pertains to learning. Some of the most interesting findings are that the environmental structure directly affects learning processes in children. The more enriched classroom environments, with multiple opportunities for experiential learning, will positively affect all students no matter what learning difficulties they may have. Brain maturation and practice are necessary for those skills that we expect most K-5 students to exhibit in some way. These are working memory, organization of information, and attention to details and specific information for the purposes of analysis and problem solving.

So what do we do with this information? Knowing how the brain works and the implications that brain function has for our teaching practices will allow us to make strategic design decisions for our classroom management, structure, and lessons. Here are some interventions to boost genius brainpower in your classroom:

1. Get up and move! Exercise boosts brainpower because oxygen feeds the brain and revs the thinking engines. Have students do something active just before teaching them (or while teaching them) something new or critical.
2. Recognize that every brain works differently, and if what you are teaching a child isn't "clicking," change what *you* are doing.
3. Helping students recognize patterns in learning rather than memorizing details is more accessible in their brains.
4. Get emotional! Events that are emotionally charged (any emotion) are more conducive for learning than those that are emotionally more neutral. Emotions are controlled by the amygdala, which helps in learning!

5. Keep your lessons short! The attention area of our brains only stays plugged in to stimulus for about ten minutes. If you need more time, get students reengaged with a reactivation of emotion.

6. Create a learning environment in which initial learning is complex, meaningful, elaborately experienced, and is mimicked in assessment situations.

7. Have them remember in small bites: To help long-term memory become accessible when needed, have students learn new information over time and build upon each new step (i.e. step 1, step 1 and 2, step 1, 2, and 3, and so on).

8. Incorporate as many senses in learning as possible. The more senses one uses to learn something, the more solidly it is stored in the brain.

9. Allow students to explore and *see* the learning in a deliberately planned discovery- and creativity-rich learning experience.

As teachers, we are charged with teaching children to become thinkers and problem solvers, not just fact-filled responders. We know that we must teach the whole child—his or her heart, motivation, curiosity, confidence. But all of those stem from the brain. We must understand how the brain functions and is structured for learning in order to teach in a way that most effectively plugs students' brains into curricular and experiential information.

The Fearless Administrator

Cultivating a fearless district where every student is given the chance to actively participate in their own learning and collaborate beyond the wall of their school with global peers takes an administration willing to be as fearless as that which I am saying teachers and students need to be. Often the pressures of politics, numbers, data, and funding create a fear-based approach to running a school. Sometimes it can appear that wanting the best for kids might be in direct opposition to what seems to be the ultimate goal of no child left behind. But, indeed, I say it is actually directly correlated. If the administration is willing to support the staff on their campus, create an environment of collaboration, self-driven accountability, ownership, and high expectations among the teachers—and if the staff buys into the idea that they are part of the solution and not the over-worked, under-appreciated, and "fully responsible for the fate of the world" people that it can sometimes feel like—then we can change the face of American education. The strategies and pedagogical ideas in this book that ring true for the effectiveness of the learning that takes place in the classroom for students also ring true for the effectiveness of these strategies when used with teachers. The fact is that everyone, no matter in what capacity they work in the educational system, must, without fail, feel like they matter. They must feel like what they are doing is purposeful, respected, and needed. We all need to feel like our contributions are not only appreciated but also necessary for the overall success of the goal, which should be to give every student in our country the opportunity to experience unforgettable learning every day. Speaking to educators on the frontline, this all may seem like "preaching to the choir." But by working together with your administration and sharing the extraordinary learning that is happening in your classroom; especially after creating a fearless classroom, you truly can inspire your leadership to grow and change, and be more open to the possibilities of innovation and change across campuses and districts. Be patient, stay positive, and keep growing! What you are doing is making a difference and changing the lives of the little geniuses in your classroom.

Creating Fearless Learning Environments

Wonder rather than doubt is the root of all knowledge.
—ABRAHAM JOSHUA HESCHEL

ICAP Rotations

I often think about why, over the past fifteen years of teaching, my classes' scores always looked the same: some excelled above grade level, most achieved at grade level, and some remained below grade level. I worked tirelessly trying to discover some magic formula to reach those struggling students. I taught my tail off, planned wonderful lessons that I taught with passion, integrated technology, and followed the traditional small-group set-up so that I could give certain kids the "extra attention" they needed. But after all that effort, I still had the same results: some excelled, some achieved proficiency, and some remained sub-par. The problem was that the ones who excelled didn't really move much in terms of academic progress and were not as challenged as they could have been, and the ones who needed to progress faster simply didn't. So I tried something new.

I needed to motivate and engage ALL of my students and to be able to concentrate on them all equally for their own differentiated needs. But how??? Who has time to meet with every single kid every single day and still teach everything expected to be taught? It was a mind-boggling and frankly overwhelming and defeating thought.

I tried several popular rotation formats and, though they helped free up some time for me, I found that I was spending more time monitoring behaviors and trying to get kids to stay on task than I was actually being maximally productive during that time. Then, over the summer, reflecting on what my students' behaviors and words had taught me, I realized I was doing it all wrong.

Students need to feel challenged and productive during the day. Give them something curious or puzzling and they engage with determination and relentless perseverance. Watch them playing games, any games, doing puzzles, anything mentally challenging and somewhat entertaining, and they will work hard to accomplish the task successfully. They need and want to use their imaginations, curiosity, and passions. So I developed the ICAP approach.

ICAP Stands for Imagination, Curiosity, Adaptation, and Passion. These are the names of the centers through which I thread my curriculum-embedded, project-based learning activities. In these centers,

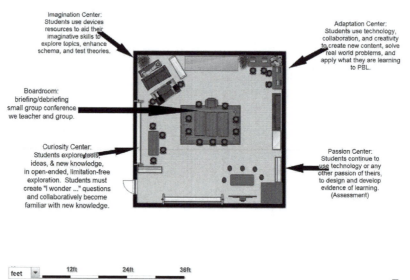

FIGURE 2.1 The Fearless Classroom Layout

Allowing constant flow and collaboration-conducive vignettes offers a learning environment rich in language, cooperation, and productivity.

students are able to experience the curriculum in ways of application and synthesis while practicing the basal skills to achieve success. They learn to collaborate and negotiate learning with each other as well as independently. These are all part of the missions in the game of our classroom culture, but I wanted to focus on the attributes of the missions more specifically. Here is a brief description and the objective for each center:

I: Imagination

Students in the Imagination Center are asked to use their knowledge to discover new information or innovations using their skills, or develop deeper connections to the content. For example, in a language arts lesson on iambic pentameter, students might be asked to rewrite a Dr Seuss story in iambic pentameter. They might be asked to write a tweet that follows the same rules. They might be expected to create a six-word figurative language caption to a photo they take using a device. Perhaps they study the molecular structure of unknown blood specimens to determine a new hybrid animal. In a math lesson about geometry, they might have to construct something out of blocks and attribute blocks in order to create a scene of their choosing. The objective is to get students to be creative, productive, and imaginative. It is to get them to use their knowledge in a way that connects with their imagination. The gamification missions in my classroom require some sort of imagination application in order to complete the mission and provide the necessary learning evidence.

C: Curiosity

Students in the Curiosity Center spend some time discussing and reflecting in wonder about the tools or concepts being learned. In a language arts lesson on contractions, students might be expected to wonder about the apostrophe and what its uses are and why it is necessary. No guided questions are needed other than simply asking them to write ten questions that they have about the apostrophe. The depth of questions they will ask will surprise you! In math, students might be asked to think about rulers and why they are comprised of 12-inch spaces, or what the smallest measurement in the world might be, or why they are called rulers in the first place. The objective is to get students to write their own lessons and to authentically buy into the content being learned. Once these "wonder" questions are written, it is up to the class as a whole to research and discuss to determine the answers to these genius questions. There are a multitude of options for discovering the answers to these questions such as connecting with experts in a field, reading books, connecting with other classrooms, and even involving community members or parents as mystery experts.

A: Adaptation

Students in the Adaptation Center are asked to use their knowledge to discover new information, create innovations using their skills, or develop new content. For example, students in language arts might be asked to develop a new rhyme scheme that evokes a certain emotion. In math students might be asked to create a video game level using area and perimeter that also teaches the player about the concepts. In science, students might develop a technique for studying rocks that streamlines the standard tests used in the field for determining a rock's identity. This is a center that lends itself nicely to collaborative efforts with experts, professionals, and global collaboration. The objective is to challenge students to think globally about how their skills might be used in different ways.

P: Passion

Students in the Passion Center are asked to express their learning through their passion. Some students are athletes, some musicians, some artists, some gamers, some writers, but whatever and whomever they are, they have a passion. This center allows them to express what they are learning through their passion's skill set and share it with others. This is also the center where our community outreach projects are worked on. The objective is to connect kids to their passions and to celebrate what's important to them.

During the ICAP rotations, I am able to connect with students individually. I confer, teach, connect, and share in the learning experience. The activities I choose are engaging and challenging, and, because they feel in more control of their learning and see the purpose in the activities, students are on task and learning constantly. They are collaborating, discussing, adjusting, and negotiating. They help each other and take ownership of not only their individual learning, but also that of the class as a whole.

The first year I began using the ICAP rotations was with a class who scored 62 percent below grade level at the beginning of the school year. By the end of the school year, our final standard assessments were 100 percent at or above grade level proficiency in math and 97 percent in reading. The data speaks for itself. ICAP has transformed my classroom, and I have been freed to integrate myself as a facilitator of learning and one who is able to meet with every single student, every single day, in an authentic learning experience and intervene in the moment.

ICAP: The Specifics

Imagination

It is important for students to practice what they are learning in real-world and meaningful ways. The Imagination Center is designed to ignite the imaginative center of their brains while focusing on the

FIGURE 2.2 Students in the Imagination Center use their understanding of geometric shapes to create an Educreations demonstration of the shapes' similarities and differences.

FIGURE 2.3 Another snapshot of students working in the Imagination Center.

content being learned. Students will practice their skills, make new connections, and face activities that will challenge them. The activities should elicit trial-and-error thinking, and failure should be expected at first.

To plan for this center, think about how you want the content to be applied to new ideas and create activities that will provide opportunities for them to discover new learning through exploration of content possibilities.

Here is an example of this planning process for a lesson in imagery:

Overlying question: How is the imagery of the tree in Shel Silverstein's *The Giving Tree* similar to the imagery of the doll in Patricia Polacco's *Babushka's Doll*?

The idea here is to get students to make connections using content from two seemingly unrelated pieces of imagery.

The objective of this lesson is to have students explore and discover the magic of imagery. Students will practice identifying, writing, reading, and explaining imagery. Using imagination, students will create images from words. In order to help them, students will be asked to select a noun and an emotion at random, and will be asked to create the emotion through words by using the noun. An example might be selecting a butterfly and the emotion anger. Students might describe the "crimson in its violently flapping wings." Students will need to dig deep and use word resources like dictionaries and thesauruses in order to reach proficient-level scores.

In a math lesson on subtraction with regrouping, students would be asked to create a demonstration of the concept of regrouping either in procedure or as a manipulative strategy.

Curiosity

The next center focuses on the students' curiosity. It is important for students to buy into their learning. Having students think about and write questions that inspire their curiosity will immediately engage them and hold their interest.

In planning this center, provide specific items about which the students will be asked to explore, ponder, and wonder. In keeping with the two sample lesson concepts from above, here is a plan for the Curiosity Center:

FIGURE 2.4 Students in the Curiosity Center create a "Wonder List" for future research.

FIGURE 2.5 Another snapshot of students in the Curiosity Center.

FIGURE 2.6 Another snapshot of students in the Curiosity Center.

In the Curiosity Center for the imagery lesson above, provide images of a variety of scenes. Provide vocabulary words that concern imagery. You want students to wonder why imagery is used, how it is used, and what if imagery is changed or omitted in a story. How are the images related to stories read? Curiosity sentence stems can be provided at the beginning of the year. Have students write questions as to why an author chooses to use certain imagery in order to convey his or her desired meaning. Have students wonder how a story might change if the imagery were changed.

In the math lesson on subtraction with regrouping, have examples of scenarios where regrouping is needed (in making change with a purchase, for example) and ask students to wonder about why regrouping is necessary.

Wisdom begins with wonder.

—SOCRATES

I really love this quote. My immediate reaction is, "YES! I want my students to not only be knowledgeable with the content I teach them, but also more than that I want my students to be wise." I want them to be wise about problem solving, the words they choose to express their thinking and feelings, and about the possibilities a healthy curiosity can provide. The second reaction I have to this quote is more of a reflection. Do I provide frequent and purposeful opportunities throughout every day in my classroom for kids to wonder? I believe that allowing students to wonder, explore, ask questions, and collaboratively develop schemata about new topics is one of the most effective ways to introduce new learning to kids.

In math, I have given students math tools (snap cubes, base 10 blocks, rulers, scales, etc.) and have asked them to explore the items openly. For example:

ME: What do you wonder about that item?

STUDENT: Well, I know it is a ruler and it is used to measure the length of things.

ME: Great! You know something about rulers! But what do you wonder about them?

STUDENT: Hmm. Why are there only 12 inches? Why not 10? It seems 10 would be a lot easier measurement to use.

ME: Good! I don't know. But I bet we can find out! What else do you wonder about rulers?

ANOTHER STUDENT: I wonder what cm means and why these are smaller marks than the inch side.

ME: Hmm. Yes! That is very curious! Let's write that down so we are sure to answer that too!

ANOTHER STUDENT: I wonder why it is called a ruler. I thought rulers were like kings and queens!

ME: Ha! You're so right! That is an interesting question! Let's write it down.

The rich conversation and learning opportunities that ensue from such wonder allows for lessons to essentially form themselves. Sure, students need to experience measuring various lengths of items in standard and non-standard units. But allowing them to explore information and to have experiences that led to discovering the answers to their wonder questions solidified their learning of the purpose of measuring length, as well as creating resourceful, curious, and validated thinkers.

Reading and writing actually lend themselves nicely to curiosity. Here is an example of how a lesson to develop character traits gave students the opportunity to curiously explore the following prompt:

"Your character is found in an embarrassing situation."

This is a departure from the old-school way of prompting, such as: "Tell me about a time you were embarrassed."

They were given about five minutes to wonder about the statement, to discuss what they wonder, and to write some thoughts down.

By allowing students to discuss their thinking with each other, they were able to not only adjust their own thinking, but also add to and broaden their own wonderment about the character.

After their time to be curious, they were asked to share some wonder questions that they had. Here are a few that they contributed:

"I wonder why my character felt embarrassed. What bothered him or her the most about it?"

"If this had happened to someone else, how would my character have felt then?"

"What if my character was given a do-over? How might they have done things differently to avoid this embarrassing situation?"

"Is there someone or something that my character could turn to for help?"

These questions helped other students focus in on the "humanness" of characters and helped them write real, relatable characters. When it was time for them to start planning and drafting their stories, these questions were the go-to resources for ideas. This was much more effective in eliciting quality writing from students than the prompts often found in state assessments.

The point is that curiosity needs to be consistently, frequently, and authentically cultivated and facilitated daily with your students across content.

Adaptation

In planning for the Adaptation Center, think about how you can provide real-world opportunities for students to explore and use their learning in meaningful ways. Connect with classes around the world for this center or even just with another class or the students' parents. Here they collaborate and negotiate to practice and apply their learning to create new content.

In the lesson on imagery, have students work with their global partner to perhaps write a Twitter imagery phrase for a specific feeling

FIGURE 2.7 The Adaptation Center allows students to research, explore, and create new content using knowledge they have and are building in the lesson.

or emotion. Ask students to write imagery scenes for their partner, who will then draw what they think is happening in the scene using specific color choices to evoke the emotion in the original prose of imagery.

In the math lesson on subtraction with regrouping, students could work together to create a demonstration of the concept both in procedure and in story problem using the app Educreations or any Web 2.0 tool.

Passion

In planning for the Passion Center, provide a task that students will be required to tackle in any way they choose. Students who are artistic may want to draw a picture or create an infographic. Students musically inclined might write a rap or song. Others will want to create videos or games. Whatever their passion, they may use it to complete the task.

In the lesson on imagery, ask students to create a passionate reading response to three examples of imagery in a text. They can use

FIGURE 2.8 Students in the Passion Center work together to create a training video to teach states of matter.

green screening, claymation, Web 2.0 tools, and any other media that will adequately convey their response to the literature.

In the lesson on subtraction with regrouping, have students explain why regrouping is needed in some cases, when to know when to regroup, and how to regroup. Create a training video or poster of sorts. The idea is to get students to passionately respond about literature or their learning rather than just journaling a response every time.

The Boardroom

Probably my favorite part of our daily learning experiences is the boardroom. After every experience we sit together in a boardroom-style setting and come together to debrief as equal experts on the topic. We share ideas, struggles, successes, failures, discoveries, and questions still lingering. This is the magical moment where every student feels validated and needed as a contributor to the greater learning of our classroom. This is when I informally assess individual learning and have the opportunity to intervene

FIGURE 2.9 Students prepare to present their findings in the boardroom discussion.

on any misconceptions. This is a special moment in class that at first was uncomfortable for some students, but, after realizing that no sincere contribution to the discussion goes unconsidered, they become eager to share and strengthen each other's knowledge construction.

Fearless Planning and Lesson Design

First comes thought; then organization of that thought, into ideas and plans; then transformation of those plans into reality. The beginning, as you will observe, is in your imagination.

—Napoleon Hill

Planning on Genius

As we mull over curriculum maps, previous years' lessons, stacks of resources and materials, we put together a plan of action that we hope will elicit the most effective learning experience possible for our students. We think about differentiation, small-group lessons, whole-group lessons, rotations and centers. We try to find solid independent work for them to do while we meet with other students. We look at what the state standards are and the student levels of expectations. We talk to each other about what we *have* taught and how we *should* teach it this year. Often we "pre-plan" and bring materials and assignments, worksheets and ideas to the planning table with our colleagues. Planning is done in a fifty-minute block with copies being flagged for the copier, books being pulled, and activities being discussed for lessons. This is a typical planning session for most elementary school teachers and possibly middle and high school as well. And it has worked, for the most part, to provide quality education for most students year after year. But what if creating a truly fearless and genius classroom actually started with the planning and that planning meant a completely new approach?

Fearlessness in the classroom consists of a fearless educator who designs a deliberately planned, idea-driven, experiential learning environment where fearless students are positively supported and are free to explore, discover, and collaborate. Here students can take academic risks and engage their curiosity and imaginations in order to form deeper and more meaningful connections to the curriculum, each other, and their world.

Planning is critical to the success of the fearless classroom concept. If one were to search the Internet for lesson plan templates, one would find millions of options out there. Most follow essentially the same idea and format:

- *Whole-group lesson or mini-lesson*: This usually consists of modeling new thinking or strategies, a read-aloud, and teacher-led instruction to learn new content.
- *Small-group lessons per student needs*: These are usually specific, guided groups to target the learning needs of individual students.
- *Centers or rotations*: These are usually games or other "hands on" activities for students to do in a circuit of learning.
- *Technology*: This usually comprises independent time with some form of technology, e.g. playing a game on the computer, watching a video or using another type of media, or interacting with an app. Usually this is a consumptive activity delivered through technological media.
- *Journal entries*: These are usually prompts of some sort where students must write a response in a journal as it pertains to what they have been learning.
- *Assessment*: These are usually pencil-and-paper worksheet-type tests that target facts which have been learned.
- Learning objectives, language objectives, and content objectives for each subject area are embedded in some of the more effective lesson plans as well.

If these types of plans have been reasonably effective in designing adequate and sometimes excellent learning experiences for kids, why would one suggest changing them? Being fearless means being able to examine with a critical eye what has worked and what hasn't worked, and being willing to make changes to even the best-laid plans so that the extraordinary can be accomplished. Certainly I am not implying that there is anything wrong with these templates. Obviously there are fantastic implications for these plans. What I am suggesting is improvement.

Below is a template I designed to help organize lesson design thinking in terms of fearless learning environments. I have also included rubrics for assessing the level of specific components. They offer suggestions for embedding those components into your plans.

Lesson plans for: [teacher name]

Duration:

Student goal setting:

Content areas covered:

State standards or common core standards covered:

Direct student learning outcome objective(s):

Indirect student learning outcome objective(s):

Facilitator guidance: Teacher acts as a learning facilitator by teaching specific vocabulary and content that will *not* be addressed in the activities. This guidance is more about how to navigate the activities than teaching content.

  Curiosity activity: Students explore without restrictions the materials pertaining to the content being taught.

- In reading, students will peruse words, sentences, text, author bios, images, and other materials that will connect to the learning objectives. There are *no expectations* on students other than that they "explore and wonder about how these materials might be connected."
- In math, students could explore a new manipulative or math tool for the purpose of wondering about it only. You would want them to write their curiosity questions in their math journals or curiosity journals.
- In science, students would use or explore science tools or experiment materials and write about what they wondered or thought about how the materials were connected.

Imagination activity: Students work together to solve science, technology, engineering, and math (STEM)-based problems or sharing ideas and learning about what they wondered or learned.

Passion activity: This is a fun one! This is an activity where students produce some sort of learning evidence based on the experience of the lesson. This could be technology-based or a piece of artwork, writing, or action. Students choose how they want to express their learning but the outcome expectations can be set by you.

Adaptive activity: This is the "What If" activity. Students address teacher- or student-written questions that require analysis and synthesis of learning. This is to predict or project future outcomes or inferred connections through comparisons or contrasting thoughts.

Assessments: Three-tiered performance assessments consisting of written work, demonstrative work, and interview.

It is recommended that students have rotations of at least twenty minutes and try to get at least two rotations in per subject area. However, because often there are many content areas that are covered in one activity lesson, focus less on teaching a specific content during a specific time and more on the activities. For the purposes of scheduling and structure, the activities are placed in content areas based on the targeted learning objective that is directly addressed with the activities.

Using this structure, the students learn together through exploration and discovery. You are there as a safety net and a guide to help them. Small-group instruction, if needed, can be easily implemented in this structure. However, if you are floating around the classroom listening and observing you can intervene frequently and target individual needs much more effectively.

#4

Fearless Grading

Grades should act as data to promote and encourage progress and excellence. If they do not, they are ineffective.

As teachers, we face the inevitable task of assigning a numerical or alphabetical value to a student's work. The higher the number or the closer to the beginning of the alphabet one's value is, the smarter one must be. This is the way it has always been. We have even identified students as "A" students or "F" students. By this definition teachers have made certain assumptions. "A" students are organized, attentive, studious, and conscientious. "F" students are lazy, distracted, unorganized, and often defiant. But, today, we know this is simply wrong.

But what does it mean, then, to get an A or 90 or a 4? If a student is "proficient" and the teacher gives him or her a 3, how much *more* does that student need to show to get a 4? This is the ever-debatable, ever-frustrating aspect of teaching: finding a grading system that promotes excellence, provides meaningful data, and allows students and their parents to glean a more accurate picture of the student's academic abilities.

Assigning Meaning

Assigning meaning to a grade that specifically defines the expectations of work is one of the most important components in developing a grading system. What does one need to do to earn an A or a 4?

Defining that this grade requires a student to work consistently beyond the level of proficiency is helpful in determining the caliber of work for this grade. If teachers use the verb in the state standard as the identifier of proficiency, then anything above that standard would constitute a higher-level grade. But what if we simply define a student's work as we do teacher work as below expectations, proficient, and exceeds expectations? Isn't this much more meaningful? Why do we use arbitrary grading systems to rate student work, and a completely separate one for ourselves?

In my classroom, I have an "Academic Profile" sheet for every student that can easily be translated to the report card so that it becomes more meaningful to the parents. If the task is "practice work," i.e. developing a skill, students simply receive a "Try Again" for below-expectations work, "Level Up" for proficient work, and "Achievement Unlocked" for exceeds-expectations work. It aligns with the gamification concept in my classroom and keeps their focus on the quality of work without getting caught up in the grade (www.fearlessclassroom. blogspot.com/2013/04/fearless-gaming-in-classroom.html). Without the gamification concept in place, students would receive a "Try Again" for below-expectations work, "Right On" for proficient work, and "Exceptional" for exceeds-expectations work.

Table 4.1 is a sample of part of an Academic Profile Sheet.

What Goes into a Grade?

I remember when I could raise my grade simply by doing extra worksheets or behaving in class. I could even replace a low quiz grade with a homework grade if I completed 100 percent of my homework. Then it seemed like a fine idea! But what is that actually teaching or assessing? If you give homework, connect it to the learning and have it be a portion of the skill requirements. Make it meaningful and purposeful to the acquisition of learning.

Quality vs. Quantity

How many times does a student have to show exceptional work in order to earn an "exceeds"? Does he or she need to be observed over time and context using the skill in higher levels of understanding?

TABLE 4.1 Academic Profile Sheet

Name: Student A
ID#: 012345
Grading Period: Beg. Date–End Date
Academic Area: English Language Arts (ELAR)

Summary comments: Student A has been learning Skill 1, Skill 2, Skill 3, and Skill 4 this grading period. He has also been improving Skill A, Skill B, and Skill C from previous grading period where he scored a Reteach or Below Expectations score. Below are his scores for these skills followed by anecdotal notes for ELAR:

Texas Essential Knowledge and Skills (TEK)	Skill and How Assessed	Exceeds	Proficient	Below	Reteach
ELAR 2.14B	Defined/ observation	X			
ELAR 2.2A	Verb/skill defined/ written journal			X	
ELAR 2.2B	Verb/skill defined/ reading conference		X		

Comments: Student A has exceeded expectations on SKILL 1 by _____. I am very pleased to see him using this skill to support his needs in _____. SKILL 2 remains below expectations due to _____ but will be addressed through the following interventions: _____. Fantastic work on SKILL 3, which is proficient! He is able to consistently use this skill with only occasional need for clarification. Skill A is now proficient as he is able to _____ where before he was only _____. These interventions assisted him in acquiring strength in this skill. Skill B remains below expectations. However, he is making progress. He is now able to _____. However, he still must _____ consistently before achieving proficiency. The following interventions will address this need: _____.

Grading should always elicit a desire for quality over quantity. If a student produces exceedingly proficient pieces of work 80 percent of the time, he or she shouldn't need to produce several more pieces just to "prove" that he or she has the skill at a high level of understanding.

Grading needs to define quality for students. They need to know what they are expected to do and how to get there. Goal setting, planning, self-awareness, and access to their data and progress, even in primary grades, allow students to take more ownership of their learning as well as giving them a clear understanding of where they are academically.

There is so much chatter in the education community about how to adequately assess where a student's academic proficiency lies.

Between standards-based grading and performance assessments and traditional grading, how can we provide ourselves, our students, and our administration with the truest evaluation of a student's academic competency?

A proper place to start is to understand what grading systems are most frequently used in our educational system and the implications of each. By understanding them, perhaps we can collectively devise a more comprehensive, well-rounded evaluation plan.

In traditional grading systems, students are given a letter or numerical grade for their performance on assessments. Quizzes, tests, reports, essays, projects, and other forms of assessments are used to determine a student's overall proficiency score. Participation can play a role in these scores and often completion of the task is given some weight in determining these scores as well. Each assessment is independent of the other and often isolated in the content it addresses. These assessments often assess only a student's ability to recall learned and consumed facts, and rarely do they ask for much productive reasoning using those facts.

Traditional grades often result in a percentage or a letter based on a percentage. Receiving a 100 percent is the highest grade a student can achieve, while a 0 percent would be the lowest possible grade. An "A" is any score within the range of 90–100 percent, "B" any score within the range of 80–89 percent, and so on. Failing is considered anything below 60 percent and in some cases 69 percent or lower. This is the grading system most of us grew up in and frankly defined ourselves in.

The problem with traditional grading is what plagues us still today: a comprehensive score doesn't identify or target specific skills that need to be addressed for the student to become more successful as he or she progresses through school. For example, if Jane receives a score of 75 percent on a reading comprehension passage, what exactly were the skills she didn't have solidly enough to be more successful? Hard to tell, isn't it? Without going through the test and perhaps even discussing every question with her, one might not know. Doing this for every item on every assessment, though essential in understanding a student's proficiency level for the objectives assessed, would be too time consuming and certainly a less productive use of everyone's time. Also, what if, as sometimes happens, the teacher doesn't get to grading the assessment immediately and time elapses? Will either the student or teacher be able to effectively remember the thought process that went into the erroneous answers? Often redos, test corrections, and other forms of retroactive grading can improve the grades on these assessments, which then skews the actual identity of proficiency.

With standards-based grading, student work is assessed based on specific objectives. Rather than giving an overall performance grade, students are given a rating for each objective. In our district, we have a form of this for elementary schools, yet return to a traditional grading system at the secondary level. At the elementary level, we score 1–4 on specific state standards in each reporting period. A "1" indicates "Not Proficient." In other words, this student needs deep interventions and constant modification and support in order to achieve success on this objective. A "2" indicates "Partially Proficient." This means that a student is beginning to show some understanding and independence but needs moderate interventions and some support in order to achieve success on the objective. A "3" indicates "Proficient." Students at this level are able to independently access skills and strategies for the objective effectively with little to no support at the expectation level set forth by the state standard. A "4" indicates "Advanced Proficiency." A student receiving this score not only effectively demonstrates grade-level understanding of the objective, but also consistently does so at the extension levels of learning.

The benefits of this type of grading system not only allow teachers and students to see exactly where a student's strengths and weaknesses lie, but also provide an opportunity for reassessment on specific skills rather than entire assessments. This makes for a much more efficient learning environment that is differentiated for each student. The student and teacher always know where the student's current levels of understanding lie for each objective.

Students in my class set weekly academic goals based on their tracking of their proficiency levels. My students use a tracking page to track their own progress. Parents, students, and I all know exactly where we are and what we are doing to find success with our goals.

#5

Fearless Assessing of Skills

Let us think of education as the means of developing our greatest abilities, because in each of us there is a private hope and dream, which, if fulfilled, can be translated into benefit for everyone and greater strength for our nation.

—John F. Kennedy, Jr.

Assessment is a crucial conversation in education today. Many wonder how educators are supposed to differentiate lessons yet standardize assessments. That is a concern for many of us and none of us has truly come up with a solid solution yet. However, we are getting closer. Performance-based assessments can be utilized to capture a more accurate picture of a student's true academic proficiency. This is because, in order for a student to create using constructed knowledge, he or she would have to demonstrate a certain level of proficiency in order to be successful.

The three-tiered approach to performance-based assessments provides a multi-modal view of a student's abilities to not only perform a task using the skills I am assessing, but also his or her ability to communicate understanding both written and verbally. First, students are asked to complete a challenge, a specifically designed task that embeds all the skills taught for that particular lesson unit. They then must write a response discussing their experience with the challenge and detailing why they chose to perform certain tasks the way they did or why it was important to consider certain facts, or how the challenge reflected the overarching question under which the skills were learned. They are then interviewed by me, or by a panel of students and me. Here they are asked clarifying questions and allowed to express any other knowledge they may have about the subject matter that they hadn't been able to express through the other two tiers. By the end of the three tiers I am able to more accurately assess their level of competency and pinpoint specific areas of misunderstanding or misconceptions. An example of this type of assessment structure is as follows:

- The overarching question is, "How do fractional parts relate to each other in terms of either a part-part-whole concept or number line components?"
- The skills being taught are:
  o Identify, describe, and model using concrete and pictorial representations of fractional parts of whole regions, sets, and numbers
  o Communicate using math language in everyday situations
  o Identify, describe, and compare 1/2, 1/4, 1/6, and 1/8 using concrete or pictorial representations.

Assessment

Tier 1—The Task Challenge: Students will create a comparative picture using attribute blocks and label the picture for fractional parts of the wholes. They will demonstrate an understanding that fractions are related to each other in terms of size and numerical ordering.

Tier 2: Students will write a response to the following statement: "Understanding fractional parts is important in studying geographical regions. Argue either for or against this statement using what you have learned about fractional parts and their characteristics."

Tier 3: Students will be given two minutes to tell me everything they know about fractions and may be subject to further questions to clarify if needed.

Students use Web 2.0 tools such as GoAnimate, Voki, and Xtranormal and Zooburst to create animated videos, speaking avatars, and

3-D animated movies to demonstrate learning. Another example of an assessment challenge over states of matter might be to have students create cartoons using the app Toontastic, where the main superhero's powers are the characteristics of their chosen state of matter and the arch-nemesis is a character who would cause an irreversible change to their superhero (such as fire burning wood).

Setting Fearless Goals

We cannot solve our problems with the same thinking we used when we created them.

—ALBERT EINSTEIN

If you have ever watched a kid play a game, especially one that required strategy or critical thinking to advance through the level, you have witnessed him or her fail over and over again yet assess, adjust, adapt, learn, improve, and eventually succeed. Even more remarkable is that kids do it without feelings of inadequacy and failure. They accept the obstacles they face as necessary to developing strong playing skills. They accept "Game Over" as an opportunity to rethink, readjust, and try again. They willingly accept, sometimes through hyper-focused attention, that frequent failed attempts are nothing more than (albeit perhaps annoying) necessary ways of achieving the inevitable success they seek. Their confidence never wavers.

How, then, do we translate the same skills into the classroom? How do we get kids to troubleshoot their own work and reproduce better, more successful attempts?

This is an uncomfortable scenario for kids because they are used to grades and points and the fear of missing recess, getting a poor score on a report card, and facing disappointing faces from teachers, family, and friends when they are less than successful on assignments. Grades are definitive and as such can be *defining* to kids. Even teachers refer to students as "A" students and "C" students or "high kids" and "low kids." I cringe when I hear the sweet voice of a teacher who is trying to sound sensitive and compassionate say, ". . . my low babies . . . ." As if "babies" negates the fact that he or she just referred to the student as *low*.

Begin from day one teaching students to assess their strengths and areas of opportunity. Do not refer to these opportunities as "weaknesses," however. Instead have students learn to own their strengths and celebrate them.

One such way to get every member of your class to embrace troubleshooting and an "all in this together" approach is to host hashtag events. Hashtag events do not have to be via Twitter though that certainly is a fantastic idea. You can use sentence strips and note cards, but, regardless of the media, students are able to share something for which they have a passion with interested peers.

Once students are able to assess their own strengths and opportunities, they need to learn to set goals. Teach students to be critical of themselves and each other with a productive eye. Help them realize that there are specific skill sets that they use daily to navigate challenges. They are thinkers, problem solvers, and imaginative beings. They need to feel as confident in these skills as those (which are often the same) that they use to successfully navigate through a game level.

After students learn to set and work toward goals, they need to be able to use data and information to assess their own work and adjust accordingly. As teachers, we can facilitate this thinking by asking questions, validating thinking, reshaping and clarifying misconceptions through guided inquiry, and sending them back to rework. I do not quantify work as proficient or below proficient by marking inaccurate answers or grades. I simply stamp "Try Again" or "Level Up." Students do not need to be bombarded with scores and points. They need to feel empowered to be able to look at their own work and determine better strategies for more successful attempts. This empowerment comes from practicing troubleshooting thinking.

Troubleshooting thinking is comprised of self-awareness and the freedom to explore other means of acquiring knowledge and success. If we are looking for cookie-cutter thinking and cookie-cutter products from students, we will continue to create a fear-laden, answer-driven environment in which students fail miserably and lose hope. The great thing about games is that a lot of the time there are multiple ways to achieve the desired goal. So, too, should it be in the classroom.

When training my students to become troubleshooters of their own work, I have them walk me through their thinking on their work. I don't indicate if they are correct or incorrect. I don't ask leading questions like "4+4 is 6? Are you sure?" A typical conference or note of feedback on a student's work is as follows:

Giving Feedback to a Student

[IN-TRAINING CONVERSATION] Math problem: 45+32=?

STUDENT: I am finished with my math.

TEACHER: Great! It looks like you worked really hard on this! I appreciate how hard you work! I'd love for you to share your thinking with me on this question.

STUDENT: Well, I knew we had been working on regrouping lately, so I figured this was going to be a regrouping problem.

TEACHER: Why?

STUDENT: Well, because I just figured you'd give us a regrouping problem so I know that I have to regroup because 32 and 5 is 37 and so I regrouped the 3 and put the 7 in the one's place.

TEACHER: Why?

STUDENT: Because you add the top number to the bottom number and if it is more than 10 you regroup. So then I added the 4 and the 3 and the 3 I carried and got 7 so the answer is 107.

TEACHER: Wow! You have really shown strong math thinking! Let me ask you a question. What might be another way we could solve this?

STUDENT: We could use a number line.

Teacher: Why?

Student: Because number lines can help add numbers together without needing to know how the procedure of adding is done.

(Student goes back and works.)

Student: Um, I got a different answer this time. I got 77 this time.

Teacher: Hmm . . . curious . . . why do you think so?

Student: I know what I did. I added the 32 and the 5 instead of adding the 2 and the 5. I carried 30 instead of just 10 and that I didn't even need to regroup 10. Once I started working the number line I realized what I did.

Teacher: Are you sure 77 is the correct answer?

Student: Yes.

Teacher: How so?

Student: Because I also used base 10 blocks to check my number line and, when I did, I saw that I would have had only 7 ones. I couldn't make a set of 10. I didn't need to regroup.

Teacher: So next time, how can you make sure you know for certain that your answer is correct?

Student: Double triple check with different strategies.

Troubleshooting Conversation Starters

- I am not sure about this strategy. How are you trying to solve this?
- I wonder if I tried this to solve the problem . . . .
- If I do this then I can do that and solve the problem that way . . . .
- Why did you solve your problem like you did?

The Five Whys

Students should be given frequent and consistent opportunities to have conversations and discussions about the work they are doing.

They need to feel validated for their thinking but also be able to learn and adjust their thinking with each other too.

After-Training Conversation on the Same Problem

STUDENT: I am finished with my math.

TEACHER: Great! It looks like you worked really hard on this! I appreciate how hard you work! I'd love for you to share your thinking with me on this question.

STUDENT: Well, I knew we had been working on regrouping lately, so I figured this was going to be a regrouping problem. I started to regroup because I added the 32 and the 5 but when I got 107 I thought it can't be more than 80 because 45 is close to 50 and 32 is close to 30 and 50 + 30 = 80.

TEACHER: Good thinking! Estimating and reasonableness are important!

STUDENT: Since I haven't been doing all that well with regrouping procedures I decided to use a number line instead.

TEACHER: Great idea!

STUDENT: I got 77 that time. I checked it by using a place value mat and adding the columns.

TEACHER: Are you sure 77 is the correct answer?

STUDENT: Yes, because I also used base 10 blocks and I counted on my fingers too.

TEACHER: Well done!

Troubleshooting is problem solving, usually to improve failed processes. It requires a logical investigation of errors so that success solutions can be ascertained. I like to give students already solved questions, published pieces of writing, etc. and have them troubleshoot if the sample is proficiently worked out or not. This is also an excellent activity for training troubleshooting thinking!

Required Skills for Troubleshooting

- Identify the "trouble" or misconception.
- Logically determine possible remedies for the "trouble."
- Experience the possible solutions to determine the most effective.
- Confirm the solution is effective through repetition.
- Learn corrective thinking to create preventive thinking in the future.

Common experiences that students are exposed to in class help form troubleshooting thinking. If they've been able to repeatedly produce the same successful results using a strategy, they will continue to use it and use it as part of their troubleshooting mental resource file. Students also need to understand that in troubleshooting it is usually most effective to explore simpler possibilities for solutions first.

A great example of this thinking is when a student is seen sitting at his desk not working. The teacher assumes he is distracted or doesn't understand. The teacher approaches and asks if the student needs help. He declines. The teacher walks away and watches as the student continues to do nothing. The teacher approaches again and asks him if she can help him understand what to do. The student says he understands. The teacher walks away again, this time patting him on the back and encouraging him to get to work. The teacher observes the student continuing to sit and do nothing. Now the teacher begins to feel frustrated and believes this is obstinate behavior. The teacher walks over and asks why the student is not working and he replies, "I don't have a pencil."

Kids need to not only have the freedom to explore a variety of possible solutions and means to success in their learning but also to meet their own needs, obtain their own resources to learn, and to speak to each other as respected resources.

Table 6.1 is a math-focused thought builder form that helps guide student thinking at first. Following it is a list of items I include in every student's toolbox that they are allowed to access any time they need.

TABLE 6.1 Problem-Solving Think Mat

Read the problem and visualize what it is saying.	*Restate the word problem in your own words.*
When I read the word problem, I imagine _____ _____.	I think the word problem is saying that _____ _____.
Identify the math language words in the word problem that help you know how to solve it.	*Rewrite the word problem using math symbols.*
The words _____ and _____ tell me that I need to _____ to solve the problem.	In math symbols the word problem looks like:
Solve the word problem. Check your work.	*Justify your answer*
	My answer, _____, is a reasonable answer to the word problem because _____ _____ _____.

Tool Box

- *Math*: coins, blocks, snap cubes, base 10 blocks, number line, hundred chart, geometric shapes, ruler.
- *Writing*: pictures, idea notebook, small items of interest, artifacts, favorite quotes.
- *Reading*: skill reminder card, self-pacing questions, question/conversation cards.

Getting Student Buy-In

I feel that the most important step in any major accomplishment is setting a specific goal. This enables you to keep your mind focused on your goal and off the many obstacles that will arise when you're striving to do your best.

—Kurt Thomas

Even the best-made plans can derail if there is no buy-in from the students we are serving. They must be invested in their own learning, and fully knowledgeable about their progress, strengths, and areas of opportunity. When a student is able to visualize his or her goals and verbalize how he or she will reach them, that student is more invested and feels more responsible for achieving those goals.

Every Monday, have the students in your classroom set their goals for the week. It takes about ten minutes for them to complete, but is worth every second of time to set their minds on their individual accomplishments and to set goals to address their needs. It is important, at first, to model with each individual student how to evaluate his or her own strengths and opportunities. At the beginning of the school year, meet with each student throughout the Monday and help him or her understand what the student is doing well and on what he or she needs to work. Discuss reasonable goals versus ambitious goals. Set three goals: two reasonable goals and one ambitious goal. The goal-setting sheet in Table 6.2 is used at the beginning of the school year to help guide student thinking and to help form their goals.

I have students first visualize and then draw themselves as they will be when they celebrate their accomplishments at the end of the week.

Once we set our goals, we revisit them each subsequent morning for about 2–3 minutes, visualizing and spending some quiet moments focusing our minds on the end goal of success. We have seen the level of goals as reasonable and the extent of ambition increase as the school year has progressed. Students are eager to accomplish their goals and it makes them feel so proud to achieve that which they set out for themselves to accomplish.

TABLE 6.2 My Goal-Setting Sheet

This week: _____.

Writing:
I am proud of _____.
I will improve _____ by _____ so that I can meet my goal.

Reading:
I am proud of _____.
I will improve _____ by_____ so that I can meet my goal.

Math:
I am proud of _____.
I will improve _____ by _____ so that I can meet my goal.

This ability to be self-aware is critical to learning as it helps students make meaningful and sound decisions about their own learning experiences. Even at the young age of seven or eight years old, students are able to be taught how to evaluate their own abilities and make adjustments to achieve their goals.

Even as we teachers use data to drive our instruction, so should our students use their own data to drive their goal setting and learning.

#7

Guide to Fearless Activities

People who use time wisely spend it on activities that advance their overall purpose in life.

—JOHN C. MAXWELL

In order to redefine a classroom into a fearless classroom, one must abandon some misconceptions. First, the notion that lesson plans are the road map to running a classroom needs to be debunked. Lesson plans should be designed with the objective and student discovery outcome in mind. The actual activities could vary from table to table, student to student, or day to day. Lesson plans need to focus on the *how* of student learning more than the *what* of student learning.

Second, planning as a team is not the physical act of discussing a shared plan that the entire team will follow. All students are different and have different ways of taking in information. Team planning should be about the desired student learning outcomes and the most efficient and effective ways of achieving those outcomes. *How* the individual students actually succeed in accomplishing those outcomes should vary among the teachers, classrooms, and student needs.

Third, we must abandon the idea that rubrics are grading systems. Rubrics should assist us in developing activities, lessons, and concepts by focusing our thinking on the specific aspects needed to achieve the desired results.

This shift in thinking will feel uncomfortable to those of us who have built a career on meeting as a team on a Tuesday afternoon with our respective content standards and materials, and sharing activities that can deliver the information. Then leaving the meeting with an "everyone is teaching this content this week this way" lesson plan.

Using Rubrics

The following are rubrics that may help in designing lessons with the end result in mind. *How* are you going to achieve the student's learning outcome you want and what if you want to include a specific component in your lesson?

Student Product Rubric

This rubric focuses on both the rigor of design of your lessons and the level of productivity of the students.

Lesson Design Rubrics

These rubrics focus on the rigor of design of your lessons.

Writing

There is a garden in every childhood, an enchanted place where colors are brighter, the air softer, and the morning more fragrant than ever again.
—ELIZABETH LAWRENCE

Genius Journal Responses

Journal writing is one of those areas that teachers either do really well or miss by a mile. There is usually no grey area on the subject. Most agree that there is a need for journaling in the classroom, even blogging, or vlogging (video blogging), but what we are asking our students to respond to is a completely subjective concept. Sure, it is important that students are able to express their learning on a topic.

"Write a quick paragraph explaining the stages of metamorphosis of a butterfly."

"Compare and contrast a square with a cube."

"How are the presidencies of Abraham Lincoln and Barack Obama similar?"

TABLE 7.1 Student Productivity Lesson Plan Rubric

Focus Area	4	3	2	1	Total
Building of Knowledge and Skills: *Students interpret, analyze, synthesize or evaluate the content. They draw inferences, make interdisciplinary connections, compare and contrast connections, and decide the accuracy of the information through research.*	The students are mostly responsible for building their own knowledge and produce work that draws inferences, makes interdisciplinary connections, compares and contrasts connections, and demonstrates the accuracy of the information through research.	The students are mostly responsible for building their own knowledge but do not produce work that draws inferences, makes interdisciplinary connections, compares and contrasts connections, and demonstrates the accuracy of the information through research.	The students are somewhat responsible for building their own knowledge but produce teacher-centered or teacher-led work that draws inferences, makes interdisciplinary connections, compares and contrasts connections, and demonstrates the accuracy of the information through research.	The students are responsible for building knowledge provided by the teacher and reproduce that information in their work.	
Integrated Technology: *Students consume, use, make decisions, and create using technology to demonstrate their learning and synthesis of their learning.*	Students actively create websites, wikis, templates, games, apps, videos, podcasts, and other Web 2.0 or multimedia products to demonstrate their learning for others to use. Students make decisions about what technology should be used and how.	Students actively use advanced Internet media such as graphics, videos, and podcasts, and create less advanced photo stories or audio recordings to demonstrate learning. Students are given a choice of a few less advanced technology options but are told how to use them.	Students use basic skills such as typing, viewing videos, playing single-player games, and using social media to communicate with others. The teacher gives the technology and use of technology to the student.	Students do not use technology to produce. Students consume information from technology only.	

(Continued)

TABLE 7.1 (Continued)

Focus Area	4	3	2	1	Total
Communication of Information: *Students communicate their learning effectively and in an organized, coherent, and accurate manner.*	Student communicates learning by expressing an original idea with clear and well-developed details that extend beyond the content expectation levels.	Student communicates learning by expressing an original idea with clear and somewhat developed details that extend beyond the content expectation levels.	Student communicates learning through clear information that extends somewhat beyond the content expectation levels.	Student communicates learning by expressing a reproduction of learning idea with some details but does not extend beyond the content expectation levels.	
Problem Solving: *Students use content to process, solve, and implement resolutions to real-world problems.*	Students use most of the content to solve real-world problems, which can be proven as successful and which they implement effectively in a real-world situation.	Students use most of the content to solve real-world problems, which can be proven as successful.	Students use most of the content to solve hypothetical problems.	The students' use of content to solve problems is minimal or non-existent.	

TABLE 7.2 Lesson Plan Rubric

Focus Area	4	3	2	1	Total
Collaboration: *Students make substantive decisions together that affect their work regarding content, procedures and processing, and the final product.*	Students equitably share the sole responsibility for the work and make substantive decisions about the content, process, and product of their work.	Students share the responsibility for the work but do *not* make substantive decisions about the content, process, and product of their work.	Students work together but do *not* have shared responsibility for the work.	Students are not required to work together and have independent and individual responsibility for the work.	
Building of Knowledge and Skills: *Students interpret, analyze, synthesize, or evaluate the content. They draw inferences, make interdisciplinary connections, compare and contrast connections, and determine the accuracy of the information through research.*	The students are mostly required to build their own knowledge and produce work that draws inferences, makes interdisciplinary connections, compares and contrasts connections, and demonstrates the accuracy of the information through research.	The students are mostly responsible for building their own knowledge but produce work that only connects to one content area regarding: draws inferences, compares and contrasts, and demonstrates the accuracy of the information through research.	The students are somewhat responsible for building their own knowledge but teacher-led/given information is the main focus and the teacher draws inferences, makes connections, compares and contrasts connections, and demonstrates the accuracy of the information through research.	The students are not responsible for building knowledge and only reproduce information through familiar processes.	

(Continued)

TABLE 7.2 (Continued)

Focus Area	4	3	2	1	Total
Student Pacing: *The time line of the lesson requires students to self-monitor and set and meet deadlines.*	The lesson or activity is a long-term activity (more than one week) and students use rubrics to guide their pacing and must plan their work in order to successfully complete the activity on time.	The lesson or activity is a long-term activity (more than one week) and students use rubrics to guide their pacing but teacher sets deadlines and benchmarks to help students plan their work in order to successfully complete the activity on time.	The lesson or activity requires students to use rubrics to guide their thinking only and the teacher paces the lesson	The lesson or activity does not require students to use rubrics to guide their thinking and the teacher does not need to pace the lesson in order for it to be completed.	
Problem Solving: *Students use content to process, solve, and implement resolutions to real-world problems.*	The lesson requires that students use most of the content to solve real-world problems, which can be proven as successful and which they implement effectively in a real-world situation.	The lesson requires that students use most of the content to solve real-world problems, which can be proven as successful.	The lesson requires students to use most of the content to solve hypothetical problems.	The lesson does not require students to use content to solve problems.	
Integrated Technology: *Students consume, use, make decisions, and create using technology to demonstrate their learning and synthesis of their learning.*	Technology is mostly used to support and build knowledge, and students *must* use technology to build that knowledge.	Technology is mostly used to support and build knowledge, and students use technology to build that knowledge but could build that knowledge without technology.	Students use technology to practice skills and reproduce information but *not* to build on their knowledge.	No technology is used in this lesson.	

These are adequate prompts for an expository of learning. However, in the fearless classroom movement, they are simply prompts for fact regurgitation. Students consume information and respond with the facts in the form of a written response. To be clear, there *is* a place for this type of writing in all classrooms. Students *do* need to know how to respond to such questions.

But are we stopping there? If so, we are falling short of what our students deserve. We are becoming a student-produced educational system and thus must allow students to be creative in their responses. They can still inject facts but responding to a deeper level of questioning will help stimulate the part of the brain that deals with imagination and creativity, problem solving and critical thinking.

"If you become what you think, what do you think you are becoming?"

"It was at that exact moment that I thought to myself . . . ."

"Which is better, a sphere or a rectangular prism? If you could be either one, which would you be and why?"

"It is said that if you give a greedy or self-centered person an inch, he or she will take a mile. If this is true, how many inches would that person take if he or she truly took a mile?"

"If Barack Obama lived during the Revolutionary War, but had all the modern understanding and political philosophy he has today, how do you think he would handle the Revolutionary War?"

These types of prompts allow students to be creative and explore the facts in imaginative ways. You, as their teacher, can assess their understanding adequately and more accurately through prompts like these.

We need to start thinking in terms of creative genius. How do we foster creativity and imagination, and take the fear out of writing for our students?

Writing is one of the biggest struggles for students these days. They can tweet and text in shorthand, they can even Facebook and blog, but actual pen to paper writing seems to be becoming a lost art. Why? I believe that technology does play a small role in the lack of enthusiasm for the written word, but I believe more that the greater blame falls on the shoulders of us, their teachers. We teach processes and mechanics in isolated lessons; we teach editing and revising as one and the same. We teach the components of good writing and the habits of good writers, but do we foster an environment of fearlessness about writing? Do we allow for creativity? Or are we scaring them into conforming to a formula of writing?

Here are a few responses by second graders responding to the first set of prompts. Following these I will include the responses by the same second graders to a couple of the prompts above.

Typical Prompt

"Write a quick paragraph explaining the stages of metamorphosis of a butterfly."

> The egg hatches and a caterpillar comes out. This is the larva stage. It eats a lot of leaves and grows. Then it makes a chrysalis. It changes inside the chrysalis. This is metamorphosis. Last it comes out and it is a butterfly.

> The butterfly lays an egg on a leaf. The caterpillar comes out and grows. It makes a chrysalis. It changes into a butterfly. When the butterfly comes out it flies away.

Genius Prompt

"If you were a caterpillar, how might you finish this sentence: It was at that exact moment that I thought to myself . . . ."

> It was at that exact moment that I thought to myself, "Oh how I wish I could jump so high I could see the clouds. They are so far away. I am stuck here in this tree and cannot do anything but eat these leaves. If only I could jump. I would jump so high the clouds would be below me! I am getting sleepy now. I need to rest. I will rest in this shell and dream of being in the clouds."

> It was at that exact moment that I thought to myself, "In just a few short weeks I will finally be a butterfly! I have to be careful to not get eaten by predators. I need to eat healthy leaves and grow as much as

possible. Then I will be able to make a chrysalis and rest. I can't wait for metamorphosis to happen to me. Oh how I want to be beautiful!"

Typical Prompt

"Compare and contrast a square with a cube."

A sphere is round. It can roll and bounce. It doesn't have corners or flat sides. A cube is square. It has twelve edges and eight vertices. It also has six faces. They are both 3-D shapes.

A sphere is round. It can roll and bounce and turn. It does not have a flat surface or any corners or vertices. A square is a special rectangular prism. It has six square faces and twelve edges and eight vertices. It can only slide. Both are geometric figures or 3-D figures with the dimensions of length, width, and height.

Genius Prompt

"Which is better, a sphere or a rectangular prism? If you could be either one, which would you be and why?"

I would prefer to be a sphere because I like to play sports and I could be a baseball or a basketball. Spheres can fit into round holes like golf holes or basketball goals. Spheres can bounce so I could feel how it is to fly for just a moment when I am in the air. I also like to roll down hills in the summertime. Spheres can roll. If I were a rectangular prism I would only be able to slide. That could hurt. When I slide in baseball I sometimes get scrapes and bruises. Rectangular prisms could get scrapes too much. They also have edges and sharp corners. If I am going to be sharp I want to be smart. People might use me as a foot rest or a chair. I wouldn't want people sitting on me. So I think being a sphere is better.

Typical Prompt

"Tell me about the time you thought about what you want to be when you grow up."

I want to be a doctor when I grow up. I want to help people stay well. I want to make people feel better and give them medicine to help them feel better. That is what I want to be when I grow up.

Genius Prompt

"If you become what you think, what do you think you are becoming?"

I am becoming a leader. I know that with hard work I will achieve my goals. I can be a doctor or a lawyer or a firefighter or a teacher. But I don't have to be anything. I can just be a leader. I can help people make better choices just by being a leader. Leaders matter and leaders make a difference. I think about how I can be the best me I can be. I can follow the rules that make our school better. I can be a good friend and stand up for what is right. I can study and work hard. If I keep my thinking positive I can become the best me I can be.

I am not the smartest kid in school; I am not the best at math. I could think these things and never get better. I keep pushing myself to understand because I know I can do it. Struggle is good. If I believe in myself I can do anything. I am a genius because I never stop trying.

I am becoming a really great student. I think positively like, "I can do this!" and "I know everything I need to know to do well on this test." I am becoming a great student because my teacher believes in me and if she does, I should.

I am becoming a genius because I think only about how I can do things and not about how I can't. I don't ever let myself think that anything is impossible. It might seem that way sometimes, but things change all the time. The world once didn't have airplanes.

I am becoming a boy who is smart, talented, and cool. In my head I think that I can do anything in school when it comes to learning. I might not get it right away, but I can muscle through as my teacher says. I think I am a kind friend and when I do nice things for others they like me. This makes me cool. I am awesome!

I am becoming someone who matters. I used to feel like I couldn't do anything right. My parents always wanted me to make 4s on my report card but I only made 3s. I used to tell myself that I wasn't good enough. Now I see that with hard work I can do anything. I can now understand fractions and poetry and technology. I never knew that my writing could win awards but this year I placed in Penguin Palooza. I am becoming someone I like.

If these examples don't drive home the point that giving prompts that elicit innovation, inventiveness, and creativity is important, I don't know what could be more convincing. These are second graders. They are so insightful and full of promise. A teacher's job isn't to teach facts, but to foster a student's imagination to explore facts in new and creative ways. These types of journal prompts will help in that endeavor.

Reflections on Learning

Knowledge is ancient error reflecting on its youth.

—FRANCIS PICABIA

As important as goal setting is to a student's growth and determination to succeed, so too is the ability to reflect upon his or her work and derive meaning, lessons, and a deeper understanding of not only the content, but also applications of that content in various contexts. This is a skill we as teachers often do for our students. But if we can embed authentic self-reflection skills into our daily lessons, our students will be able to take their learning full circle and a sense of satisfaction of one's own growth will be theirs to savor.

How do I Embed Quality Reflection Practice into my Lessons?

These practices can and should be done during and after lessons. Your students will become more proficient and efficient with their abilities as they are exposed to these opportunities.

1. Debate it!

One of my favorite ways of having my students demonstrate learning and reflect upon their own learning is through debate. Have students argue how their understanding is an adequate summation of the content learned. In doing so, students are not only having to show that they do have a firm understanding, but also how what they have taken away from the lesson adequately covers the most important aspects of the topic.

2. Report the News!

My students love to video themselves. This is a great way to engagingly assess their learning. Have students take on the role of news anchor and report "Today's Hot Topic," and provide a quick overview of the content in the lesson.

3. More than Two Ways

As students work together on collaborative groups, have them include in their reflection all of the ways they could explore the content and still arrive at the same conclusion. For example, in a group of four students working on a project about recycling, each student will approach the learning in his or her own unique way. As they learn to express their own thinking with confidence, this reflection skill will enhance their ability to not only identify and own their own thinking, but also be able to develop an empathetic view of the thinking of others.

4. Mingle and Merge

After students complete a lesson, have them mingle around the room looking to merge with 2–3 other students who have a different perspective on the content. They are to link up with those students to form a more comprehensive perspective. As students mingle, they gain stronger understanding and learn more information that might have been missed. They have to present the group's understanding of the content, giving credit to the contribution of each member.

5. Mingle and Match

Similar to Mingle and Merge, students are asked to mingle around the room searching for 2–3 students who share their perspective on the content. They are to link up with those students to form a united group who will then argue that their understanding or findings are comprehensive, logical, and repeatable.

6. Put the Art into Smart!

Most students enjoy artistic expression, even if they are not the best artists. Have students create a visual expression of their learning. They may draw, illustrate, or construct a depiction of what they have learned.

7. The Rubric Has it

Traditionally, rubrics have been used to assess understanding or as guidelines to create projects. In this exercise, students use a rubric to assess each other's thinking. Points such as "Is your partner's thinking logical?" and "Does your partner's thinking use creative thought when coming to his or her conclusion?" help students observe the thinking of others in a more critical way and thus enhances their own thinking.

8. Examine and Experiment

After a lesson has concluded, have students reflect on their learning by taking what they consider the most interesting aspect of the content and examining it further and on a deeper level. They will then develop an experiment that will test their "wonder question" about the topic.

9. Solve it!

Create a problem or situation that needs resolution in which students are required to use the content they learned to solve it. Genius journal prompts are a great place to start thinking about these kinds of scenarios.

10. Act it Out!

Reflection doesn't always have to be in written form. Students can play a game of charades or put on a one-act play demonstrating their learning.

11. Tweet it!

Twitter is a fantastic way to share concise learning reflections. If your class has a Twitter account or if each student has a Twitter account, you can storify their reflections as a sort of virtual learning portfolio. Having students tweet their reflective thoughts about learning requires them to have a full understanding of the content and challenges them to pack as much reflective thought as possible into 140 characters.

The idea is to not only have students identify their strengths and opportunities as learners, to set attainable and realistic goals that reflect this self-awareness of skills, but to also have the opportunity to frequently examine their thinking and learning reflectively. As teachers, we want them to be able to judge for themselves whether they are learning everything they need to learn in lessons. Conferring with students weekly also helps teachers shape this reflective piece so that students are guided toward better goal-setting and stronger learning in the future. It is a heavy task to ask of elementary students, but if they begin to practice these skills in the primary grades they will be better equipped to make effective decisions about their own education in middle and high school, and in college. The trick is for teachers to clearly set their expectations, give students feedback, and allow students to be active participants in their own feedback.

Getting Students to Ask Fearless Questions

The art and science of asking questions is the source of all knowledge.
—THOMAS BERGER

Students are generally taught to ask specific questions that elicit specific factual answers. These questions—the who, what, when, where, and how questions—help students to sort facts for the purpose of answering explicit questions about content. This type of questioning is adequate for those purposes. Students should be able to use their skills with these kinds of questions to research the facts they are seeking, to answer using a variety of resources.

However, if we want our students to be problem solvers and critical thinkers, if we want them to analyze and synthesize information for the purposes of finding solutions to unique situations or to innovate common situations, we must teach them to ask fearless questions knowing that some of their questions may not have obvious or clear solutions, and some may not have answers at all.

We need to teach students to explore the possibilities of learning more than the absolutes.

What Exactly Constitutes Fearless Questioning?

Fearless questioning is those questions whose answers come from wonderment, curiosity, discussion, and imagination. They are those questions that elicit a conversation or debate, where minds converge on a topic, mull it over, examine it from all angles, and even reconsider the purpose of the topic as it pertains to new thinking and possibilities. In my classroom hangs a large red craft paper heart with the word "WHY?" written in large black letters. This is simply one example of a question that if strategically asked can open up the entire world for a child.

The following scenario is a typical answer-driven classroom Q&A:

TEACHER: We just read *Charlotte's Web*. Who is the main character in the story?

STUDENT: Wilbur and Charlotte.

TEACHER: What was the main idea of the story?

STUDENT: Wilbur learns how to be a good friend and the delicate balance of life.

TEACHER: When did Wilbur meet Charlotte?

STUDENT: Before the fair.

As you can see, there are absolute answers to these questions and not much debate or conversation is elicited with these questions. Sure, we want students to be able to determine the answers of these questions, but these are "Bing" questions. I suggest that, if the answer to your question can be answered with a quick Bing search, it isn't a fearless question.

Here I have inserted fearless questions into the same scenario in an idea-driven classroom:

- Who do you think is the most influential character in the story? Why do you think so?
- Is it possible for nature to teach lessons of the human spirit?
- Can you think of an example from your own experiences?
- Why do you think E.B. White chose to write about farm animals to tell his story?
- What if Charlotte lives at the end? How might the next chapter read?
- What do you think it would take to convince people in real life that Wilbur should have been spared? Do you think people would believe their eyes if they saw writing in a web?
- How is Charlotte similar to Fern?

As you can see, these questions demand a thoughtful response that could require discussion and debate among your students. It is critical that we allow our students to have those conversations and to expand their answers collaboratively to glean the most comprehensive response.

Another definition of a fearless question is that it elicits *only* discussion and *remains without* an answer. For example, during a lesson on polygons, students are asked, "What is the highest number of sides a polygon can have and still have at least two pairs of parallel sides?" Students work, draw, discuss, debate, refine, and challenge their thinking, but may not come up with the correct, absolute answer. Who cares? The discussion and learning through the exploration of possibilities and trials is far more rich and valuable than defining the polygon by its attributes.

How to Embed Fearless Questions into Your Classroom Curriculum

To create a fearless, idea-driven learning experience in your classroom, implement the four Fearless Centers (Curiosity, Imagination, Passion, and Adaptation) and place Fearless Question cards in each center to get students talking. Plan out specific questions you want them to discuss, or that you want specific students to consider, and ask them in your one-to-one time as you float around the classroom. Most importantly, however, is to teach students to ask these questions for themselves. You do this by modeling this kind of questioning and showing them how valuable and limitless learning can be through questions like these.

What could happen if our classrooms were fearless, question rich, idea-driven, passion-filled perpetual conversations where students engaged in respectful and empathetic debates and discussions where the only limitations come from the need to reluctantly move on to a new topic?

Language Arts/Reading

A man's character may be learned from the adjectives which he habitually uses in conversation.

—Mark Twain

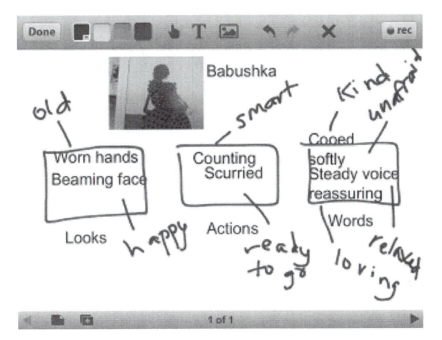

FIGURE 7.1 Students work with the Educreations app.

When learning about character traits in English Language Arts (ELAR), integrate character traits into science with pet rocks as well as characters in, for example, Patricia Polacco stories. ICAP Centers can produce incredible technological expressions of a deep understanding of character traits.

Have students use the app Educreations to create digital graphic organizers.

Curiosity Center

Choose a character from one of the books we read. Think about what their fifth birthday was like. Why do you think their birthday was as you imagine it to be? How did that birthday shape who they are today?

Imagination Center

Take a picture of your favorite character from one of Patricia Polacco's books. Import it into WordFoto and write ten character traits for that character. Save that image to the camera roll. Import your

Wordfoto image into Comic Touch and create a thought and a speech bubble expressing something that character would think and say based on his or her character traits. Add a caption that explains the character's traits as you see them. Save the comic to the camera roll and email it to the teacher.

Figures 7.2 and 7.3 are examples of the work from the Imagination Center.

Collaboration Center

Work with a partner to create a VoiceThread using your character trait images or make your own. Retell a Patricia Polacco story using these images. I am looking for your retelling skills.

Adaptation Center

Switch character traits between the two main characters. For example, in *The Art of Miss Chew*, have Miss Chew's character traits switch with those of Trisha's. How does this affect the story? What if Miss Chew visited Babushka and played with Babushka's doll? How do you think the doll would behave?

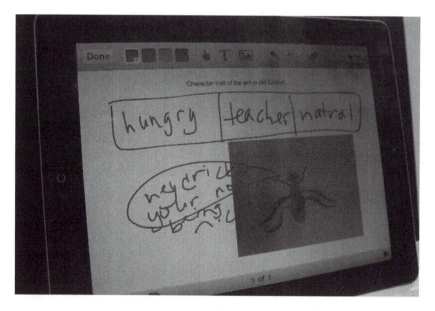

FIGURE 7.2 Connect students with their own character traits with this fun and engaging activity.

FIGURE 7.3 Students in math Imagination Center create comics to demonstrate an understanding of the attributes of geometric shapes.

Math

There are two possible outcomes: if the result confirms the hypothesis, then you've made a measurement. If the result is contrary to the hypothesis, then you've made a discovery.

—ENRICO FERMI

Measuring in The Land of Inch: *Game it UP!*

The story of *The Land of Inch* is taken from Pearson/Scott Foresman Investigations material in Grade 2, Unit 9 on Measurement. The idea is to get students to understand linear measurement as it pertains to customary units of measurement (inches) and why it is important to measure things with consistent standard units. To extend the lesson have students use Web 2.0 tools to discuss their understanding.

But as with all things education, one must continue to try to innovate and make one's lessons better and more meaningful for kids.

In conjunction with the fearless classroom approach of ICAP Centers, here is a very engaging lesson. Here are the plans and results of our work with linear measurement:

Week 1: Students will read *The Land of Inch* story.

The Land of Inch is far, far away. In this miniature land, there is a beautiful (and brilliant) princess who lives in a castle with her father, the king. One day, the king asked that all of the athletes in the land see who could jump the farthest. Unfortunately, all of the athletes measured their jumps with different units. Some measured using blocks, others with sticks, some with their feet, and others with pieces of paper. No one knew who won because they couldn't compare the distances!

Then Princess Funer noticed a pile of bricks by the castle door. She had all of the athletes jump again and they all measured their jumps with bricks. They could now see who the winner was because they were using a standard measuring tool.

The people of the Land of Inch loved this and started carrying bricks with them all of the time to help them measure things. Soon, though, they realized that bricks are heavy and lots of people were complaining of aching backs. So, Princess Funer decided to trace the bricks on paper and give out pieces of paper that were the same size as bricks—but were a lot lighter to carry. She called these papers "Inch Bricks" because they lived in the Land of Inch.

ICAP

Imagination Center: Build a house out of Legos that has the following measurements:

- Exterior wall has a perimeter of 36 inches and a cubic area of 180 cubic inches.
- One interior bedroom has an area of 24 square inches.
- One interior living room has an area of 18 square inches.

How many Legos did you use?

Curiosity Center (Rulers): Look at your measuring tool. What are you curious about? Think about how it is constructed, used, and labeled. Think of past, present, or future uses. Write ten curiosity questions that you would like answered over the course of our measurement study unit.

Adaptation Center: Broken Ruler activity: You have various lengths of items and a bucket of broken rulers. You must measure the items using only the broken ruler and respond as to the strategies you used to determine the length.

(*Teacher notes*: Some rulers are broken in half with both inches and centimeters showing but just not from "1." Some are broken down the middle showing only centimeters and will be used to measure in inches only.)

Passion Center: designing levels, paths, and houses on paper with Minecraft. *Planning phase*: Using the activity pages from your student activity booklet, called "Paths in the Land of Inch" and "Buildings in the Land of Inch," design a plan for your Minecraft World. How will your level be laid out? What materials will you use? How will you construct the buildings? Note: Each Minecraft brick or space is considered an inch.

Activity Pages

Paths and building measurements:

- Path from the king's castle to his garden is 15 inch-bricks long.
- Path from the king's castle to Princess Funer's castle is 25 inch-bricks long.
- Path from the king's castle to Pim's house is 28 inch-bricks long.
- Ren's house is about as tall as the seat of your chair.
- Pim's house is about as tall as your desk.
- Gar's house is about as tall as the doorknob is from the floor.
- The king's castle is about as tall as the bookcase.
- Princess Funer's castle is about as long as the table.
- Tob's house is about as wide as your desk.

Mini-Games

1. MathPickle.com—Dot to Dot Measurement. (Dot to dot pictures without numbers. Students must measure the distance between dots to determine if the distance matches the given target distance. If it does the student connects the two dots. A picture forms from the correctly connected dots :-) SUPER COOL!!!)

2. MathPickle.com—Perimeter and Area PolyAnimals: Students cover pictures of animals with attribute blocks and tell the area of the animal based on the blocks, i.e. this butterfly has an area of eighteen triangles. Then they measure the sides of the shape created by the attribute blocks when creating the area and determine the perimeter. They must also write the equation for each side's number that solves the perimeter question.

Reflections in Writing

Must be taken through both mathematical and writing processes. Due at the end of the unit (two weeks).

1. It has been said, "If you give her an inch, she will take a mile." This idiom speaks to someone being given some freedom and taking it farther than expected. If there are 12 inches in a foot and there are 5,280 feet in a mile, how many inches are in a mile?

2. In ancient times, the body ruled when it came to measuring. The length of a foot, the width of a finger, and the distance of a step were all accepted measurements.

Inch: At first an inch was the width of a man's thumb. In the 14th century, King Edward II of England ruled that 1 inch equaled 3 grains of barley placed end to end lengthwise.

Hand: A hand was approximately 5 inches or 5 digits (fingers) across. Today, a hand is 4 inches and is used to measure horses (from the ground to the horse's withers, or shoulder).

Span: A span was the length of the hand stretched out, about 9 inches.

Foot: In ancient times, the foot was 11 and 1/42 inches. Today it is 12 inches, the length of the average man's foot.

Yard: A yard was originally the length of a man's belt or girdle, as it was called. In the 12th century, King Henry I of England fixed the yard as the distance from his nose to the thumb of his out-stretched arm. Today it is 36 inches.

Cubit: In ancient Egypt, a cubit was the distance from the elbow to the fingertips. Today a cubit is about 18 inches.

Lick: A lick was used by the Greeks to measure the distance from the tip of the thumb to the tip of the index finger.

Pace: The ancient Roman soldiers marched in paces, which were the length of a double step, about 5 feet; 1,000 paces was a mile. Today, a pace is the length of one step, 2 and a 1/2 to 3 feet.

Given these facts, choose something larger than a pencil in the room and measure it in as many of these units as possible.

- Inch = 0.083 feet.
- Foot = 12 inches.
- Yard = 3 feet or 36 inches.
- Mile = 5,280 feet or 1,760 yards.

3. Near and far.

- Around the earth (at the equator): 24,901 miles.
- Across the continental US: 3,000 miles.
- From the earth to the moon: 238,854 miles.
- From the earth to the sun: 93,000,000 miles.

a. How far is the moon from the sun according to these measurements?
b. About how many continental USs can span the earth at the equator?

ICAP (Week 2)

Imagination Center: Create something that can fit into the following spaces using only Legos. (These spaces are created using cut-out spaces from card stock. Students are expected to measure the hole and apply the measurements to construct something that will fit.)

- A 3×5 inch rectangular space.
- A 2×8 inch parallelogram-shaped space.
- A 4×4 inch square space.
- A 6×9 inch rectangular space.
- A 7×10 inch parallelogram-shaped space.
- A 1×1 inch square space.

Curiosity Center: Students explore maps, housing blueprints, capacity containers, and graduated cylinders to wonder how measurement is needed on those items. How and why are scales utilized to reduce greater distances?

Adaptation Center: Develop a measurement scale system for this map (a local road map). How would you scale the distances? Why do you think your way would be more effective?

Passion Center: Minecraft levels development: Students create Minecraft levels using their plans from last week.

Mini-Games
Continue with the Math Pickle games.

Reflections in Writing
Finish answering the three questions from last week. *Due* at the end of this week!

Minecraft Level Assessment
Students were asked to take me on a tour of their level, discussing perimeter, area, cubic area, and measurement using academic vocabulary and accurate calculations and equations. They were assessed on the comprehensiveness of their mathematical work and the creativity used in developing their levels.

The requirements are:

1. Define in both equation and measurement the distance length of each path between each building.
2. Define in both equation and measurement the square inch area and perimeter of the garden.
3. Define in both equation and measurement the cubic area of each house.
4. Describe up to five special features you added to customize your level.

Fearless Parent Relations

Each day of our lives we make deposits in the memory banks of our children.

—Charles R. Swindoll

It is a critical part of a fearless classroom to create respectful and constantly connected relationships with the parents of the students in your classroom. There are few greater commitments you can make than committing to your students and their parents that you are a third of the team who will provide the highest-quality learning experiences possible.

Here are some ways to make sure students' parents feel that they are a pivotal component of their child's educational experience:

1. Commit to send email updates weekly that not only highlight what was learned, what will be learned, and what is happening in class, but also feature student of the week and digital examples of student work.

2. Have students create weekly vlogs (video blogs) for their parents that address glows for the week of what they are really proud of accomplishing, and grow that they really want to work hard to accomplish next week. They then offer a suggestion to their parents about how they think their parents might be able to help them at home.

3. *Twitter*: Make a private Twitter account for your class that parents can follow. Have students and parents tweet back and forth throughout the day. The rules are that every tweet must address a learning question or answer—no personal chitchat.

4. Video tape yourself talking about "news" from your classroom and send the video as a twist on the weekly emails. Parents *love* this!

5. Have an Instagram account that is private and only parents may follow. They have a chance to see daily pictures of activities that happen in class. Assign three "Instagrammers of the Day" daily.

6. Highlight students of the week in their own celebratory GlogsterEDU and send it to all parents.

7. Create an initial report card instructional video to help parents understand how to read and understand the grading system in your district.

8. Have Facetime Friends every Friday, where a parent can Facetime read with their child.

9. When you will be out of the classroom, create an interactive wiki and/or Skype with your class to keep them involved.

As long as you are honest, make an effort to include the parents, and through fearless education and respectful interactions give their children the very best opportunities to learn that you can, you will have no problem keeping everyone happy and engaged in the betterment of your students' lives.

Fearless Gaming in the Classroom

Man is a gaming animal. He must always be trying to get the better in something or other.

—Charles Lamb

The notion that struggling and failing is important to learning runs counter to traditional approaches to US education. In fact, failure and its accompanying "F" grade stigmatizes a student as unprepared or "challenged" and is usually seen as a predictor of failure in future grades. In the world of gaming, however, the very elements of struggle, challenge, and failure that discourage kids in the classroom become the primary drivers of engagement and achievement.

Transforming my classroom into a living video game was a response to knowing that engagement in the classroom is essential to learning and that challenges like those in games are what we humans are wired to need. Indeed, we crave brain stimulation and even the most straightforward games can provide that.

How to keep the attention of students is an ongoing topic of conversation among educators. When students are interested in something, they demonstrate a powerful ability to maintain focus on even the most challenging tasks. Case in point: video games, which are so challenging that players fail 80 percent of the time—and yet the players are still motivated to persevere. If we can tap into even a fraction of this energy and enthusiasm we can affect the kind of educational transformation called for in the 21st century.

I began the transformation of my classroom by looking at the curriculum and writing storylines that would challenge students to solve science, technology, engineering, and math-related scenarios. For example, one such storyline under the reading content area is "Explain how two given scientific conclusions are similar, and identify which of the scientists we've studied might have written these conclusions based on textual evidence." A math example storyline is "How are fractions connected to the concept of multiplication?"

I use QR codes and augmented reality codes to help students move independently from one activity to the next (see www.visualead.com). Kids use cell phones or tablets to scan the barcodes, which take them to websites or instruction pages with directions for the next activity, or to "cheat codes," with strategies to help them solve the "boss-level problem" (Qrafter is an example of an app that scans barcodes, and is available on iTunes).

Students are active players in their own educational game. In the past I have had each player create an avatar (Marvel, Lego, Diary of a Wimpy Kid, DoppelMe, ClayYourself, M&Ms) that can be upgraded as students unlock features by mastering skills and levels, and earn digital badges. But these, albeit fun, novelties didn't enhance engagement. The challenges were what held their attentions and ultimately raised their competency levels. (The avatar creators I listed above can be found at these sites: http://marvel.com/games/play/31/create_your_own_super-hero; www.reasonablyclever.com/mini-mizers/mini-mizer-2–0; www.wimpyourself.com; www.doppelme.com; http://clayyourself.com; and www.mms.com.)

Technology is an essential and critical component of my classroom and is used in an organic and authentic way: as a tool to find information, synthesize content, and create learning evidence to ultimately "beat the level." Students also use technology to collaborate and discuss what they're learning.

This method of delivering content requires a "letting go" of the stage, but not control of the classroom as it might initially seem. The activities are rigorous enough for my students to be challenged and engaged, but not so difficult as to frustrate them to the point of quitting. Integrated into this type of learning strategy is an ongoing review of previously learned skills, as point values are given to every activity—and, even if kids succeed in "leveling up," they are compelled to return to a previously "mastered" skill activity and try to beat their score.

I spend approximately 30–45 minutes a day in direct whole-class instruction. The rest of the time I am facilitating thinking through monitoring their work by asking pointed guiding questions. It takes more meticulous planning on my part to create the codes and activities that elicit independent thinking and collaborative work, but the payoff in student behavior, self-esteem, motivation, and determination is well worth it.

We are not preparing students for the world of today or the careers of even the future as we know it. We are preparing them for the world they have yet to create and the jobs they have yet to conceptualize. Personal learning experiences are essential to the fearless classroom approach and to transforming our educational system into truly 21st-century learning environments.

Beginning to gamify your classroom can feel overwhelming at first. I recommend that you gamify one aspect of your classroom at a time. This way, you will become more proficient with tools and streamlining instruction in this new way of delivery and will not feel bogged down in the maintenance of an entirely gamified classroom experience.

How to Begin

First of all, understand that it isn't the complexity of the game, nor the graphics and bells and whistles, that make games fun for everyone. It is simply the challenge of accomplishing something that we perceive as doable with hard work or practice. Our brains are hard-wired to react favorably to challenges. We can, however, shut down or want to give up if the task seems too challenging or impossible. So, your first order of business should be to figure out what your end goal is and then work backwards from there. Games are highly motivating to kids and they become authentically engaged in gaming situations, willing to collaborate, work beyond their comfort levels, and achieve at higher levels than when asked to do the same skill in a non-gaming situation. As teachers, we know that games such as Angry Birds or Flappy Bird can be a distraction in class. My question is, why? Why are they more interested in playing a game that requires little more thought than trial and error rote play where a simple swipe of the finger across the screen achieves the desired results? Why is the content in class less interesting? Simply put, it is boring and lacks challenge. In Jane McGonical's book *Reality is Broken* she refers to the game of golf. This analogy resonated with me as I began to take the leap of faith into the gamfication of my classroom. She writes about how golf is conceptually a simple game. The objective is to put the ball into the hole. So, she asks, why do we not just simply take the ball, walk up to the hole, and drop it into the hole? We would achieve 100 percent accuracy every single time! Mission accomplished! But we don't. As a matter of fact, we actually did quite the opposite. We decided that dropping the ball into the hole is boring. What is the fun in that? So we put the hole as far away from us as possible. We added obstacles like sand traps and water hazards, trees and gullies. We even made these clubs that we had to use to hit the ball toward the hole. We made it more *challenging*. We made it a game. The curriculum and delivery of that curriculum has for far too long been asking students to do nothing more than pick up the ball, walk to the hole, and drop it in. Students no longer care to pick up the ball.

We need to make clear the difference between gamification and gaming. Gamification uses game elements such as missions, challenges, badges, points, levels, and unlockable achievements to engage students in learning the content of the curriculum. Gaming is using actual games in innovative ways to promote productive learning. Game-based learning can include board games, online games, and game console games to reinforce and create productive learning opportunities for students.

Examples of Gamification

Players Unite!

The first thing my students receive as they enter my classroom is a user's manual that is the instructions for how to play the game of my classroom. Here is an example of such a brochure: http://xbrox360.wikispaces.com/home.

This is actually a great opportunity for a final project for your exiting class to create for your incoming students or, better yet, a first project for your new class so that they can have a voice in how their game will look! Allow your students to collaborate on designing an instructional manual for how your class works. Have them write the narrative of the storyline and the objectives and rules for playing the game. This brochure can easily be revised and newer versions of the game can "be released" as the year moves forward and you change and grow as a class of players.

The beauty of having your class collaboratively participate in the designing and creation of their instructional manual is to give them ownership of not only how the class will operate, but also ownership toward the goals, outcomes, motivation, and procedures. Allowing students to work together and share ideas also evens the academic level playing field for students, so that students who might otherwise struggle with academics in a traditional setting might find strengths and opportunities to shine through leadership or imagination that might not otherwise be discovered.

If you want to truly transform your classroom through gamification, you must develop a storyline. The storyline from my classroom is as follows:

The Department of SIOG Training (SIOG = Significantly Important Operational Geniuses) is enlisting the help of my genius students to help them fight the evil-doings of the Voiceless. The Voiceless is an evil entity trying to stifle genius thinking in children everywhere. It is up to these genius students to collaborate with empathy and compassion in the missions set forth from the Department in order for them to solve the cases and bring the Voiceless to justice!

Knowing the Lingo

Before you can gamify, you need to know the language to use so that you can successfully recreate the gaming world in your own classroom. Here are just a few examples of gaming terminology that you can use throughout your gamified classroom and lesson design:

- *"Newb" (NoOb)*: someone who is inexperienced in gaming or new to the gaming world (newbie).
- *PvP*: player vs. player.
- *Avatar*: a digital representation of a player.
- *MMG*: Massively-Mulitplayer Game—a game with other classrooms playing along with you. Massively-multiplayer is a multilayered game that includes more than fifty players (at least in this context).
- *Game Master*: in this case, *you!* This is the teacher and he or she controls the game.
- *Mod*: modification. This is often an enhancement that makes a game more fun. Students can help create and suggest mods for your game.
- *Hacking*: in this case, hacking would be cheating.
- *Co-op*: Cooperative play.
- *XP*: Experience Points. Students can earn these as a way to level up.

Level Up or Try Again

Part of what makes a gamified classroom fearless is the opportunity to embrace failure as a natural stepping-stone to success. Students know that, in the gaming world, their failures do not prevent them from succeeding. They see phrases like "Try Again" and "Game Over" as just more chances to learn and adapt their strategies to find a better approach to successfully completing a level. And in our classrooms, just like it is in video games, we must allow students to get do-overs and second chances. Part of this requires us teaching them that it is okay to fail as long as they are troubleshooting their work. They must participate in discovering what went wrong and how they can adapt to find a better solution. If the teacher is the one telling them what they did wrong it defeats the idea of allowing them to adapt their thinking. We as teachers can help them evaluate their work by asking them questions like, "What was your thinking here?" or "How did you get that answer?" or "Why do you think that answer might not be the correct one?" In the same vein of thought, however, gamers often return to successfully completed levels to try to "perfect" the level or improve their high score. This same goes for those students in your class who successfully complete a task. You may give them a choice to "level up" or to improve their score! This allows students to truly take pride in the work they do yet feel capable of improvement.

What is most important here is that students are able to evaluate their work and to decide for themselves how far they want to take their own learning. It builds a natural self-competitive characteristic in students that will promote intrinsic motivation as they progress through school. It combats the instant gratification that is experienced daily in almost everything we do. Students learn that sometimes they will have to work hard to achieve something and that it may not happen for a long time, if at all. That is a life lesson that every student needs to learn. Best of all, the pressure of failure is completely removed and failure becomes essential to ultimate success.

How do students level up? There are a variety of ways students can level up in a gamified classroom. They can level up by completing missions or quests, or by earning a certain amount of points. Design your leveling system to reflect the storyline of your classroom game. This could be similar to the rankings in the military or a class-created ranking system. However you design it, make it meaningful and engaging to the students who are playing the game.

How leveling up looks in your classroom depends on the overall level of gamification in your classroom. Leveling up in a badge reward system can occur when a student collects a specific amount of badges or earns a certain special badge, like a golden badge for example. Students might earn a specific amount of points (these can be life points, stars, XP [Experience Points], or any other form of point delivery system) in order to level up. You can combine these two level-up requirements so students have to not only earn points but also badges.

Power Bar!

How and when you give feedback to your students is critical, but it can also be challenging to figure out how to do this effectively without driving yourself crazy. I suggest taking a look at games and how they offer feedback to the player and then trying to develop a system that is easy to administer and isn't greatly time-consuming.

Observing how games tell players if they are succeeding or failing during play often takes the form of a bar or scale that indicates that the student is gaining or losing points, life points, or something similar. Regardless of the way it is presented, it is crucial for the player to know how he or she is doing throughout the play of the level. It is a challenge for classrooms to work this way because you would essentially have to know what every student was doing every minute of every day. That simply is impossible. But it is possible to provide an adequate amount of feedback to the student to allow him or her to adjust and reevaluate their work prior to turning it in or taking an assessment. We can do this by allowing students to provide feedback to each other and facilitating that dialogue through structured models and support. In my classroom, students work together as guides for each other. They know not to give answers or even lead too much with their feedback or questioning. I have taught them how to provide thoughtful and constructive feedback, and to ask questions like "Why?" and "How?" to elicit discovery of better solutions by the students themselves.

In our classroom we have student progress bars on each desk or table space. This is the student's own indicator of how he or she is progressing through the level. Students must complete tasks successfully. They earn bonus points for behavior such as collaboration and cooperation. Students can always go back and attempt previously successful levels to increase their points. These points do not reflect grades or proficiency. There is no correlation to grading. It is simply an indication of progress. This is a gamified way to set individualized and attainable goals with students, and have them keep track of their progress. When struggling students see an end nearing to the level, it motivates them to push through and keep trying.

Quests for Home!

Using technology creatively can easily transform your classroom into a game, including the idea of homework. I am not a huge fan of homework for the sake of homework. I believe that it should be a natural extension of the classroom learning environment. Whether you are flipping your classroom or assigning projects, homework needs to be purposeful and engaging. Students should *want* to do it. One way you can gamify homework is through social media like Twitter. Send a quick mini-challenge out to your students and have them reply via Twitter to a designated hashtag. Assign special letters or numbers to each challenge or assignment/project and have students determine the secret code to unlock an achievement. Use QR codes or augmented-reality codes to transform the delivery of content at home. Have students scan their codes to find out what is next in the quest or challenge.

Choose Your Own Path

Using the ICAP rotation center for Passion, you can give your gamified classroom players a voice in their assessments. Students can unlock the bonus level of choosing how their learning is expressed. For example, instead of taking a pencil and paper assessment, students can choose different expressions to demonstrate their understanding of the curriculum. By allowing students to be creative in their delivery of their own knowledge and skills, they take more pride in their work and this gives them a chance to express their understanding at higher levels of proficiency. I use QR codes and augmented-reality codes to transition students throughout the level. Each code offers a choice that leads to a different yet equally challenging conclusion. By offering choices throughout the learning adventure, students are always encountering novelty and curiosity as to where their learning will take them. This ensures engagement and a willingness to push through difficult tasks.

Badge of Honor

Digital badging is a staple of gamification. It can become quite a daunting task if you are assigning them on a site such as a wiki as I did when I began. I created them, designed them, uploaded, and awarded them.

This was a time-consuming yet extremely effective method of rewarding students for their work. But I quickly realized that badging was an extrinsic motivator and that the focus needed to be less on collecting badges and more on the challenges themselves. Sure, badges are a good ways of acknowledging student achievement and can be used as incentives for students who are difficult to motivate. There are sites that provide the opportunity to automatically award badges to students after successfully completing their work, such as Edmodo and 3D GameLab.

Technically Gamified

Using technology streamlines the process of gamification, though it isn't necessary to make a successful transition to gamification. We are striving to teach 21st-century skills in our educational system, however, so it is important that we at least consider the use of integrated technology. Keep in mind that students are already proficient in the use of technology in their everyday lives. There are many good sites that help teachers customize their gamified classroom management like ClassRealm and ClassDojo. You can award points to students for anything from being student of the week, to being on time, to doing extra work, or being a good friend. Other resources you might want to explore when choosing a technological approach to gamification are Gamestar Mechanic and 3D GameLab.

Gaming

Using games in the classroom is another way to innovate and create an engaging learning environment. Traditionally games are consumptive experiences. Players play, learn, and practice skills, but often are not asked to create with games. Using ready-made games online is a fantastic tool for assessing learning, inspiring student-created products, and enhancing learning. I have included three examples of how I have used the Game Up section of Brainpop.com as productive learning experiences in my classroom.

MasterMines

The premise of the game MasterMines is to search for rock and mineral samples in the "field" and bring them back to the lab for testing to determine what your sample is. As you advance through the game, more tests become available for you to use. This game is phenomenal for teaching the various attributes for rocks and minerals. My students brought in rocks from their own homes and I gave them a rock or mineral to use as well from our campus science lab. Part of the curriculum is to describe and identify rocks and minerals based on attributes. Students used the game as a training tool to learn how to conduct each test and how to think about the results of each test with regards to classification of the sample. After testing one mineral for luster, color, hardness, and streak in the game as a model, I sent the kids off to conduct their own experiments on their rocks and minerals. They conducted the luster test, color, streak, and hardness tests for themselves, and then sorted their table group's rocks and minerals in order based on certain criteria. They even explored their rocks and minerals under a microscope for a better idea of classifying them. This activity was a fantastically engaging experience that provided deep understanding and a higher level of exploration than other possible activities I have done in the past.

Thrillin' Game: Coaster Creator

During our force and motion unit, it is important that students experience and experiment with different force and motion components to determine how the environment affects the different forces in action. One of the experiments I have done in the past is to have students build marble roller coasters out of everyday materials. Part of the problem with this activity is limiting the materials and having some of the materials ruined or destroyed before the coaster can be built because the natural trial-and-error aspect of such an activity doesn't allow for limiting materials. Using Coaster Creator allows students to digitally experiment with the true content being learned, force and motion, without ruining the materials while testing out their theories.

This is the activity:

- Give pairs of students the challenge to get a marble to roll the distance of a foam runway. Encourage them to find a variety of ways the marble can travel this path by changing the position of parts of the runway.

- Students use Coaster Creator to explore and research in simulated form the possibilities of their design.
- Students create their own coasters using one marble, five 8-inch pieces of masking tape, and five foam tracks (pool noodles cut in half) *only*.
- Students are given points for ingenuity, creativity, and inclusion of a variety of coaster features such as loops, turns, and slopes.
- Students use Coaster Creator to discuss their findings with the class.

A "Gutsy" Assessment: Guts and Bolts

During our study of the systems of the body, students learn each individual system and its purpose in the human body. They learn how and why the systems connect to each other and work together and affect each other. Guts and Bolts is a game that has students connect pipes from one of Moby's systems to another. It begins very basically and becomes much more complicated as the game advances. While students play the game, I have asked them to turn the volume of the game off and to screencast themselves playing. I expect them to talk me through why they are connecting the systems the way they are and to use the proper vocabulary and any other learned facts. They essentially become little doctors during this assessment!

Here is the activity:

- Students learning about the body systems are asked to determine the flow and connection of the systems to one another.
- Students explore a variety of activities to introduce and teach the separate body systems and how they function.
- Students are asked to create a diagram connecting all body systems together.
- Students use Guts and Bolts as an assessment tool. Students screencast themselves playing the game and explaining what they are

thinking. They must use the appropriate vocabulary and explain why they are connecting the systems the way they are.

Using games as productive activities can engage students at higher levels of thinking and enhance the level of understanding.

It isn't about integrating technology well, or being the most innovative educator on the planet. It is about giving students unforgettable personalized learning experiences every day. It is about opening the door to experiences that your students might not otherwise have the opportunity to enjoy. We have these young minds for a limited time. It is up to us to maximize every single moment we have to create opportunities for students to engage in the most incredible learning experiences possible so that they learn not only the curriculum, but also to believe in possibilities, hard work, and themselves . . . fearlessly.

#10

Globalizing Your Classroom with Fearless Project-Based Learning

Free the child's potential, and you will transform him into the world.
—MARIA MONTESSORI

How *The Tale of Despereaux* and Choosing to Matter Brought Fearlessness to a Whole New Level of Genius

I was quite serendipitously presented with a thoughtful question one night on social media. Angela Maiers asked, "How big is your brave?" This was a question that I immediately felt would be interesting to bring to my third graders. Even more perfectly coincidental is the fact that we just began reading *The Tale of Despereaux* by Kate DiCamillo as a novel study this week. Book One discusses light vs. dark, perfidy and bravery, and judging someone's differences unfairly. This question of how big one's bravery is was a perfect tie in! On the drive to work this morning, the radio hosts were discussing "the world's most difficult question to answer." The question, they said, is, "What is your favorite feature about yourself?" The discussion explored how confidence tends to be viewed negatively in our society and that young people, especially young girls, are taught early to keep such musings to themselves. Sure, we are capable of showering others with compliments, but to actually compliment ourselves can be tough. What will others think? How would we be perceived?

I began thinking that this too might be an interesting conversation to have with my third graders.

So when my Fearless Geniuses walked into class the following morning, we finished Book One of *The Tale of Despereaux*. We analyzed theme, discussed characters and their traits, learned new vocabulary. We empathized and shared how the story affected us as we read. Then, I unveiled these two writing prompts:

1. What is your favorite thing about yourself? What is your favorite physical feature and why? What is your favorite "heart" feature and why?
2. How big is your brave?

They had the opportunity to not only support their thesis statements by discussing textual evidence from the book, but also to explore a deeper examination of themselves. The results of this highly engaging writing assignment are as follows:

Abby

In *The Tale of Despereaux*, Despereaux is judged because he has big ears, is small, and was born with his eyes open. Even his family judged him. These are things that made him special and different. When I think of my own physical features I think I would choose my hair as my favorite. It is curly and I always think it is funny when girls with straight hair curl their hair to make it curly and girls with curly hair always want to straighten it to make it straight. I love my curly hair. I can wear it back and show my face or I can wear it down and show off the curls. Either way I feel pretty.

Despereaux also has a different kind of character. He sees the world as some place beautiful and not dangerous. He enjoys the light and music and a good book. He loves with all of his heart and no matter what. He is a lot like I am in this way. I am passionate about my education but I am also passionate and loyal to my family and friends. I would not commit perfidy against any of my family or friends. I am compassionate and would help them rather than betray them. Despereaux is very brave when he speaks in front of the king and professes his love for the princess, when he faces the Mouse Council, and when he finds himself all alone in the dark dungeon. His brave is very big. My brave is not that big. Sure, I can speak to people from other countries and classes and even give speeches in front of my own friends, but I also have a hard time being brave enough to really put myself out there and take risks when it comes to my work. I know I am smart. I am a genius. But being fearless is tough sometimes. I still get scared, but when I decide to push through it I always end up feeling a little braver than before.

Camaren

Despereaux was made fun of a lot. Just because he had differences like big ears and being small everyone looked at him differently. I don't think I look different from other people much. What I do like about myself are my hands. My hands can do a lot of things. They can hold a baseball bat and hit the ball far. They can write my thoughts and tell my stories. My hands can help a friend feel better. My hands make my mom smile when they hold hers. Despereaux is a kind and curious mouse. His heart is innocent. He doesn't understand why others don't like him. I am kind too. When I play sports I am a good sport and tell the other players good game no matter what. I try not to get mad when other people are not nice to me because being fearless means to find opportunities to set an example. I know that my kindness makes the world a better place. Despereaux is a very brave mouse. He has a lot more guts than he should being so small. I think it is his confidence that makes him so brave. He believes in himself. I have learned that even though things can be challenging at times, I am capable of figuring it out. My bravery has grown since being in the fearless classroom.

Ava

I think I am brave because I will stand up for myself and my friends. I have been brave for the past two years in class because I have had to work really hard and sometimes it wasn't easy at all. I am brave when

I go on stage to sing in front of a lot of people. I am strong and coura-geous. My brave is my song.

Eco-Conscious Project

On Earth Day, we took our learning and celebration to a new level. With our campus-wide recycling projects turned in, scored, and awards handed out, we focused our sights on learning and exploring why recycling is so important and how recycling can make a new world for us. This important eco-minded lesson incorporated real-world application of understanding and a creative way of integrating technology. The ICAP rotations were utilized to maximize student learning and productivity by giving students a chance to truly experi-ence the content from a variety of angles.

In the *Curiosity Center*, students explored various items made from recycled materials and were charged with trying to figure out what materials were used to create the new items. Here is a list of examples of items you might want to include in this center:

- A sleeping bag made from recycled plastic.
- A purse made of recycled plastic.
- Eating utensils made from recycled aluminum.
- A mosaic tile made of recycled glass and cardboard.
- Pencils made from recycled paper.

Students examined each item and, using their learned skills in problem solving and analytics as well as their understanding of recycling and eco-friendly actions for preserving our planet, they collaboratively created their estimations and presented the reason-ing behind their thinking using scientific reasoning, vocabulary, and research-based explanations. All of these skills would have been pretaught.

In the *Imagination Center*, students were asked to watch the BrainPop.com video on "Recycling" (www.brainpop.com/technology/scienceandindustry/recycling/preview.weml). Based on the informa-tion they learned, they were to respond to the following prompt:

"If Moby had to be recycled, what would you suggest he be used to create?"

Students wrote responses in their scientific "Discovery Journals" using grade level-appropriate conventions and mechanics, and *scientific reasoning, vocabulary, and research-based explanations*. Here are a few sample responses from third graders:

> "If Moby had to be recycled I would be sad. I knew that sometimes we have to recycle things we really love though. I would want him to become toy cars and I would like for them to go to the kids in that town where that explosion happened. They don't have toys anymore and every kid needs toys."

> "If Moby had to be recycled I would want him to become Iron Man. He could help protect us and make us feel safer in the world."

> "If Moby had to be recycled I would want him to become cans. We could fill the cans with food and drinks and send them to the people in West Texas. The explosion burned all of their food up. It would be nice for him to help them that way."

> "If Moby had to be recycled I would want him to be a musical instrument. Music makes me happy and I would want him to be a part of that."

In the *Passion Center*, students were asked to create a public service announcement (PSA) for recycling using their iPads and the apps Videolicious or Video FX. Students had to collaboratively create a script and minimal props to design a clever and creative way to promote eco-friendly habits and practices.

In the *Adaptation Center*, students were asked to view common items and come up with a new use for them. This is an extension of the Curiosity Center and required students to look at common items and to think innovatively and creatively to design new, eco-friendly uses for them. Here is a list of suggested items that you might want to include in this center and some of the suggested uses that elementary-level students gave for them:

- Use a blow dryer as a cubby for supplies.
- Use a shoe as a planter.

- Use Capri Sun bags for making totes.
- Use headbands as hooks for heavier items.
- Use soup cans as piggy banks.

This lesson, as well as the centers, can be adapted for any grade level. Think of ways you can utilize the ideas in this lesson and the approaches in each center to enhance the learning of environmental concerns. For younger grade levels, limit the items and choose high-interest, well-known items for the Curiosity Center and Adaptation Center. For older grade levels, bring in items less familiar to the students to expose them to new thinking and innovative uses of recyclable materials. For the Imagination Center, younger grade levels could watch BrainPop, Jr. videos or a teacher-made video. For older grades, have an expert Skype in to speak to students about recycling. Contact your local home improvement store for ideas about recyclable materials and their uses. For the Passion Center, younger students can create short videos using their devices or have them just simply act out a short skit. For older grades the sky is truly the limit. You could have them create stop-motion animation videos, team up with a local organization to actually produce awareness videos in a campaign, or create 30-second spots to submit to local broadcast stations for play!

Global Literary Festival
The Internet is becoming the town square for the global village of tomorrow.
—BILL GATES

In my quest to shatter the walls of my classroom and bring to my students the experiential learning opportunities they deserve, I ventured out and sought classrooms seeking to do the same for connections. I happened upon ePals.com and began working their Smithsonian Classroom Projects first (www.epals.com/projects/info.aspx?divid=smithsonian_home). I wanted to get my feet wet with "in-house" projects first before trying to connect with global classrooms. Our work with the Smithsonian was so successful that my students' www.iluvearth.wikispaces.com project was a national finalist in the Siemens We Can Change the World Challenge in 2010 (www.wecanchange.com). We were also recognized by the World Wildlife Fund for a Prezi on endangered tigers (http://prezi.com/

n6swoj2dspup/tigers). I am now a member of the Smithsonian Center for Education Board of Advisors helping to shape the Smithsonian Learning Quests program (http://shout.smithsonianquests.org). All of these resources are a great place for any grade-level teacher to begin his or her search for globalizing projects.

Look for inspiration anywhere! The award-winning "I Love Earth" project began when I received an email from my campus administration letting the staff know that we had exceeded our budget for copy paper and we were not even a month into the second semester. I personally questioned why as our district provided such technology-rich teaching and learning environments. I shared the email with the class (at the time I was teaching second graders), and they were immediately inspired to act. They researched ways to go paperless, designed a campaign explaining why it is important to go paperless when possible, and created an interactive experience for visitors to their webpage.

This project created change on both a local and global scale as classrooms from all over the world visited their webpage and began to take the pledge to change how they used paper in their classrooms. We then submitted the project to the Siemens We Can Change the World Competition and gained National recognition for their efforts.

Ready to expose my students to global experiences beyond virtual field trips, I posted an ePals project requesting participation in our Magic Tree House Global Literary Festival, which was chosen as one of sixteen Microsoft Partners in Learning projects to represent the United States in Prague, the Czech Republic, at the Global Forum in November 2012.

This project began when our campus had to cut some reading programs and I wanted to give my students a unique and motivating experience that would make reading authentically rewarding and enjoyable. I chose a book series appropriate for the grade level I was teaching at the time, but this project could easily be adapted for any grade level. For secondary grade levels, you might select a genre or a book series of their choosing; a high-interest, age-appropriate series of books. You might also choose a multicultural list of books covering the same topic to allow for your global partners to engage in a cultural exchange with your students.

The idea was to have all participating classrooms read the entire *Magic Tree House* book series throughout the school year (keeping in mind that the groupings would have to be flexible given the differing calendars and time zones throughout the world). Students would be grouped heterogeneously with partners around the world and be required to engage in an online weekly blog discussing the book they were reading at the time. Then, at the end of the project, they would work together with their global group members to create digital projects expressing what they learned in their favorite book from the series.

More specifically, participants in this innovative reading collaboration were committed to reading the *Magic Tree House* series of fiction and non-fiction companion books by Mary Pope Osborne. Throughout this journey, they shared the joy of reading with students around the world from different countries. Students shared their book analyses through blogging and included such connections as: reading responses, book analysis, author studies, and more. They were also engaged in a multimedia collaboration and competed with each other in expressing their literary experience using Web 2.0 tools, gaming, and community service projects. Students worked together in mixed groups from around the world and submitted their work for judging. The winners of the multimedia fair received a spotlight on the My *Magic Tree House* wiki as well as certificates and a My *Magic Tree House* prize!

Global Writing Project

Another project my students have created and implemented was the Write Our World Project (http://wowwriteourworldwow.blogspot.com). Write Our World (WOW) was started because I wanted to inspire my students to not only love to write, but also to find a purpose and voice that could be heard around the world. WOW is a globally collaborative project where classrooms across the world participate in writing stories that address social concerns such as childhood obesity and bullying. My students created a survey that was sent out to our global connections and to my Twitter following requesting participation. The survey asked students to submit suggestions to storylines by asking, "What breaks your heart?" Participating classrooms were given a topic about which to begin writing. The initial classroom began their story. Strong leads, setting, character development, and posing the problem were all part of the initial process. When ready, the beginnings were sent via SkyDrive or Dropbox to the country or classroom next on the randomly predetermined list of participants. I met via Lync Meeting with the other participating teachers to decide the order of circulation.

The next classroom in the cycle then read the beginning of the story and continued it from their cultural and regional perspective, and with their ideas of a possible solution to the problem. Once this part of the story was complete, it was sent to the next classroom and so the process continued until the stories found their way back to the original authors. These completed stories offered the authors an opportunity to witness the power of words, life experience, and a globally empathetic approach to solving problems. The goal was to spark a dialogue among young people that would allow them to feel like the significant and important contributors to the betterment of the lives of others that they are.

Global Social Empathy Project

This writing project, WOW, sparked yet another global project that required research, collaboration, and communication with students from around the world in a social empathy project. After reading the stories generated by the efforts of children everywhere, my students were so moved by the compassion they read in the stories that they wanted to do even more! They wanted to create an experience for kids everywhere to be able to find the same kind of compassion and support. Thus, the Heart Code Project was begun.

The Heart Code Project, found at www.theheartcode.wikispaces. com, is a gamified experience where kids can participate in missions to learn about local resources to help them deal with the things that "break their hearts." The participant developers of this project were a global group of genius elementary students who coded video games and provided research-based resources to "recode the breaking heartbeat of the world."

Students used country codes to research specific governmental or community-based resources for children, and, if nothing was found, then culturally accurate coping strategies for students in specific regions. Through this project, anyone can offer resources for their own region and participate in the missions so that children in their region may find the support they need. See an example of a student brochure in Figure 10.1.

The ICAP rotations were implemented during this project to facilitate efficient learning experiences and task completion. Here is a sample of what a day looked like for my students:

I: Imagination: Engage in imaginative thinking with your group to develop a storyline solution to the main character's problem in the global story. How would you recommend he or she resolve his or her conflict? Why do you think your resolution is appropriate and fair, or is it? Be sure to paint a vivid picture of your scene so that future readers cannot tell that your contribution was submitted separately from the original draft.

C: Curiosity: Why do you think your global partners chose their topic on which to begin their story? Research your partners' part of the world, local resources, and possible cultural viewpoints that could have affected their decision. Write, research, and answer at least ten "wondering" questions.

A: Adaptation: Plan, design, create, and execute a Minecraft, Kodu, or Scratch game that reflects the storyline and resources/coping skills you discovered through your research. Use the provided rubrics to assist you in your plans.

P: Passion: Reflect on your interactions with your global partners. How do you think you made a difference in their lives? How did they make a difference in your life? What big ideas or lessons did you learn from your experience in this project? Keep a journal of these reflections to remember small "a-ha" moments. Create a digital representation of your reflections to submit at the end of the project.

Students worked collaboratively, cooperatively, and compassionately with other students around the world to develop stories and games that tackled some fairly heavy subject matter for young people. They learned to be empathetic and respectful, patient and kind. They

Resources:

You will find all of your resources online at theheartcode.wikispaces.com

You will be required to communicate via blogging and email on ePals wiki that was set up through your registration for this project. Keep in mind that this is a global mission and that time zones may be a factor. You will be working collaboratively with students from around the world so an understanding of diversity will be necessary. In your registration packet, you received a "Code Breaker" packet and Mission Journal. Use these resources to help you stay on task.

Phases of the Project

Phase 1: With Our World

Contribute to the Write Our World stories via www.writeourworldwow.blogspot.com

Phase 2: The Heart Code Missions

Participate in the Heart Code Project Missions and collaboratively design, create, and code a game based on your collective research.

Phase 3: Future Gaming

Contribute to the gamification of future missions by submitting storylines, Web 2.0-created guides, or other components.

The Fearless Classroom
Fearlessclassroom.blogspot.com

The Heart Code Project: The Game
Theheartcode.wikispaces.com

Joli Barker
McKinney, TX, USA

The Heart Code Project

The Official Game of The Fearless Classroom

CLASS 3.0

Game Changers

Re'**CODE**'ing the Heart of the World ... One Beat at a Time!

Department of SIOG Training

Welcome, young SIOG, to the Department of SIOG Training. You have been specially chosen for your genius thinking and compassionate problem-solving skills. The world is under attack and we need your help! The Voiceless, the evil entity that is trying to stop genius thinking, is busy trying to destroy the hopes and dreams of children around the world and it must be stopped! We have come to you because you are enough. You have influence. You are the change we need. Will you please help us?

Dept. SIOGT

Your Mission ... should you choose to matter:

As a SIOG (Significantly Important Operational Genius) your mission is simple: Recode the world's heartbeat before the Voiceless Regime takes over and silences us all for good.

There are cries for help all around the world. Your mission is to listen to their needs, provide support, and create a plan to resolve the conflict before the Voiceless finds you and destroys your chances.

Your missions will take you all over the world where the young people are being overrun by the destruction of the Voiceless.

Show the young people that they matter and help them rise above the army of the Voiceless. Teach them the ways of a SIOG.

Hurry! You have no time to spare! The fate and heartbeat of our world is depending on you! You will need to equip yourself with your research team and Code Breaker Guide. We are all counting on you, young SIOG.

If you fail, our world will flat-line and the rule of the Voiceless will silence us forever. It is all up to you now. Go. May the Genius of SIOG be with you.

FIGURE 10.1 Student Brochure for the Heart Code Project

had to research culture, resources, and ideas in several places of the world. We found a purpose in our learning that far exceeded the original objective of writing a collaborative story with global friends.

The overall sentiment was that, as humans, we tend to unite in the things we hate rather than uniting in the things we love. These students wanted to make a statement that the world they wanted to create was one united in compassion and tolerance for differences. This was their voice being lent to a worthy cause derived from their passion to make a difference,

The Four Fearless Ws (and an H) of Difference Making

One person can make a difference. In fact, it's not only possible for one person to make a difference, it's essential that one person makes a difference. And believe it or not, that person is you.

—BOB RILEY

As we approached the International Dot Day (www.thedotclub.org/dotday) and through our discussions of Habitudes by Angela Maiers and the Choose 2 Matter movement, I wanted to bring to light for my students that anything we want to accomplish, we can. (For Habitudes, see www.angelamaiers.com/2008/10/classroom-hab-2.html. For Choose 2 Matter, see http://choose2matter.org.) One of our English Language Arts (ELAR) topics revolved around fiction, story arcs, and writing good paragraphs, but I wanted to connect their learning to an opportunity to commit to matters in our community. Thus, the "Four Fearless Ws (and an H) of Difference Making" was born.

Who

Who we are is essential to the difference we will make. Who we think we are may or may not be who we authentically are, but embarking on a journey to making a positive difference in the lives of others most certainly will shine a light on one's true self. So I asked my fearless geniuses this question:

"*Who* are you? Look beyond the obvious answers of 'I'm a third grader. I am a girl. I am a soccer player.' Look inside. What will your mark be on this world? You are the dot that will become the artwork of our future. Your thoughts, dreams, hopes, passions, and genius matter and will make a significant positive impact on at least one other person. You've already changed me for the better. Just by what you've accomplished in my classroom over the past two weeks, you've already taught me so much about how to improve as a teacher. So again, who are you?"

As a class we brainstormed *who* we are and decided on one name that collectively encompassed who we felt we were or wanted to become:

GENPACT (GEN for Genius and PACT as the combined ending of IMPACT)

What

Think twice before you speak, because your words and influence will plant the seed of either success or failure in the mind of another.
—Napoleon Hill

What we do and say directly impacts another person whether we mean for it to or not. Even a simple look can change a person's mood from sad to happy or *vice versa*. So I asked my class how they wanted to impact the world this year. "With passion, ingenuity, commitment, and a fearless determination to succeed, we can accomplish anything we put our minds to," I said. "So what is it that you would like to accomplish this year? It can be anything you want. Think about what would fill your heart and make a difference in the life of at least one other person."

They brainstormed, discussed, became active and alive with excitement about all the possibilities of things that they wanted to accomplish this year. We wrote down every option and then narrowed them down to two fun, "just for us" projects and three "just for the world" projects. Here is what we committed to accomplishing:

Just for Us

- Build a working go-kart.
- Publish a book.

Just for the World

- Organize, lead, and carry out a Military Care Package event to send a minimum of 100 care packages to our servicemen and women.
- Raise $20,000 for Relay for Life in honor of four staff members who are cancer survivors and countless other family members and friends we have lost to the disease.
- Raise awareness about global slavery with a focus on child slavery through technology and social media.

When

Once one sets a goal, one must also make it measurable and set a time line. By giving yourself a deadline, you work harder and stay focused on the task and goal at hand.

- We want to be published or at least have our book submitted to a publisher by March 15, 2014. We want to have the $20,000 raised for Relay for Life by Banquet Night, which should be in February.
- We want to have our go-kart built by May 10, 2014.
- We want to have our technology projects for the global slavery awareness project completed by April 2014.
- We want to have the Military Care Packages completed and sent to arrive on or before December 25, 2013.

Why

Why we do or say something is arguably more important than the word or action itself. It is from our intention that we determine the ultimate effects of what we do. It determines not only how the difference we make is perceived and received, but also how we, ourselves, receive the effect. We must choose to matter based on our passions and a genuine desire to make positive contributions to our community and not on possible recognition or reward. This is a difficult term to resolve when you are asking children, with all their wide-eyed, untainted, hopeful dreaming minds, to determine what is really driving their want to participate in these projects. So I asked them, "*Why* do you care?"

- Regarding the go-kart: "It would be cool to actually build something like that together. Can you imagine? All of us working on something that big and then being able to ride it?! Besides, we could maybe donate it to a shelter when we are finished so that other kids could ride it."

- Regarding the published book: "Why don't we write a book about kids for kids . . . about how we all matter . . . about how no matter where we come from, live, what we have, how we look, we can do something special."

- Regarding the military packages: "I would be really sad to be away from my family especially if my life were always in danger. It would make me feel good to help [a serviceman or woman] feel like they were appreciated."

- Regarding Relay for Life: "We have lost a teacher, Mrs Barker's husband, a fourth grader, and grandparents, cousins, friends, aunts, uncles, brothers, and sisters to cancer. We have a counselor, many teachers, and several students on campus who are survivors. Our school has really been affected by cancer. We want it to end! We have never raised that much money as a campus before. Wouldn't it be cool to hand over a check for $20,000 just from our class?!"

- Regarding the Slavery Project: "I saw something on the news the other day about children in another country who were slaves! I thought slavery ended when they were freed by President Lincoln! I talked to my mom about it and she said this happens a lot in other places and that I should feel grateful. I do, but I want to stop it from happening to anyone."

How

How are we going to accomplish all of these wonderful goals? It is great to dream and wish, but how can we realize our dreams? This too is a tough question to process for a third grader. In a culture like ours, with instant gratification a norm, I anticipated a shallow discussion. Shame on me for underestimating the power of a passion-driven conversation. I asked, "This is all well and good, but how in the world are we going to accomplish all of this?"

Their response?

"How can we not?"

We committed to accomplishing these goals through thoughtful collaboration, communication, diligent hard work, and fearless determination. I committed to creating projects that address our TEKS but also connect to our goals.

We are ready.

We are passionate.

We are . . .

FEARLESS!